KU-349-108

SINGING A *S*ONG OF FAITH

Daily Reflections for Lent

Edited by NANCY E. HARDY

Reflections by TRISHA ELLIOTT, MARK GIULIANO,
NANCY HARDY, ROBERT PIKE, MARTYN SADLER,
DONNA SINCLAIR, AND PATRICIA WELLS

UNITED CHURCH PUBLISHING HOUSE

SINGING A SONG OF FAITH
Daily Reflections for Lent

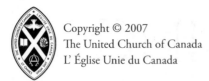

Copyright © 2007
The United Church of Canada
L' Église Unie du Canada

All rights reserved. No part of this book may be photocopied, reproduced, stored in a retrieval system, or transmitted in any form or by any means electronic, mechanical, or otherwise without the written permission of The United Church of Canada.

All biblical quotations, unless otherwise noted, are from the New Revised Standard Version Bible, copyright © 1989, by the Division of Christian Education of the National Council of Churches of Christ in the United States of America. Used by permission.

Care has been taken to trace ownership of copyright material contained in this text. The publisher will gratefully accept any information that will enable it to rectify any reference or credit in subsequent printings.

Library and Archives Canada Cataloguing in Publication

Singing a song of faith: daily reflections for Lent /edited by Nancy Hardy; reflections by Trisha Elliot ... [et al.]

ISBN: 978-1-55134-156-9

1. Lent—Prayer-books and devotions—English. 2. United Church of Canada—Prayer-books and devotions—English. 3. Devotional calendars—United Church of Canada. I. Hardy, Nancy II. Elliott, Trisha

BV85.S56 2007   242'.34

United Church Publishing House
3250 Bloor St. West, Suite 300
Toronto, ON
Canada M8X 2Y4
416-231-5931
www.united-church.ca/ucph

Design: Graphics and Print, Joyce Cosby

Printed in Canada
5 4 3 2 1   11 10 09 08 07   060281

CONTENTS

INTRODUCTION

"How can I keep from singing?" asked Robert S. Lowry in the hymn "My Life Flows On." (*Voices United* 716) The grace of God experienced in all facets of living brings song to the hearts of people of faith.

When "A Song of Faith"—poetically expressed core understandings of faith for our time—came before the commissioners to the 39th General Council held at Thunder Bay in August 2006, they voted overwhelmingly to welcome and acclaim this elegant and moving contemporary statement gathered up by the church's Theology and Faith Committee.

Whenever a small group seeks faithfully and in consultation with many to articulate what Christians hold dear and true, their task is fraught with risk. We often hear that faith is too personal a matter for anyone to try to express it. But being the church—the community of faith—we do value others' efforts to say and often sing what we believe and experience in our relationship with God.

In the United Church's 81 years, we have been blessed by risk takers willing to put pen to paper on all our behalf. The Articles of Faith of 1925 and the Statement of Faith of 1940 reveal our historic understandings, as do the ancient "Apostles' Creed" and "Nicene Creed." The United Church's "A New Creed" of 1968 has graced both personal reflection and communal worship for almost 40 years. And now, "A Song of Faith" is blessing our collective lives.

Concise creeds and clear faith statements don't encapsulate all we believe, but they are a summary and serve as maps for walking the journey of faith. In church language, they are called "symbols." Their purpose is to invite deeper reflection and evoke more profound insight into the shared way of Christ for our day.

In the pages that follow, seven contemporary writers have taken the risk to share their personal reflections on "A Song of Faith." Their gifts are offered here as a way of inviting all on the Lenten pilgrimage of 2007 to pray, reflect, meditate, sing, and act on the basis of this new communal expression of faith.

The Worship Office in the General Council's Support to Local Ministries Unit commends these pages for your devotions. We thank God for the work of these writers: Trisha Elliott, Mark Giuliano, Nancy Hardy, Robert Pike, Martyn Sadler, Donna Sinclair, and Patricia Wells. Special thanks to Nancy Hardy for her expert labour of love in editing this blessed volume to timely completion.

A. H. Harry Oussoren
Executive Minister
Support to Local Ministries/
Faith Formation and Education
The United Church of Canada

The full text of "A Song of Faith" is found on page 141.
Where lines from "A Song of Faith" are quoted, the text is italicized.

PREFACE

We've been singing our faith for a long time. "How can we sing the Lord's song in a strange land?" lamented the Hebrew people lost in their Babylonian exile. "The Lord's my shepherd, I shall not want," sang a shepherd boy on the hills of Palestine. A hymn from the early church proclaimed that "at the name of Jesus every knee should bend…and every tongue should confess that Jesus Christ is Lord." (Philippians 2:10, 11)

Whenever something earth-shaking happens, people sing. When Black slaves made their way to Canada through the Underground Railroad, they sang spirituals to bolster their courage and pass messages to one another. During the American civil rights movement in the 1960s, people sang, and when we demonstrated against the war in Vietnam, we sang again. In 1994, when Archbishop Desmond Tutu voted in his very first South African election, he didn't just sing; he danced! And today, whether it's poking fun at arrogant political leaders or protesting against injustice, we're still singing.

In the church, we sing what is deepest in our hearts—about God's creation and God's grace; about Jesus who is our friend and saviour; about the Holy Spirit who encourages us and blows us into the world. As we sing, we learn our theology: what we think and believe about God and one another. We may forget what we learn in Sunday school, but we don't forget the words to those hymns: "Jesus Loves Me, This I Know," "Here I Am, Lord," "Breathe on Me, Breath of God." We sing them, and somehow, with the singing, our faith is strengthened.

It's no wonder, then, that when the United Church's Committee on Theology and Faith responded to General Council's request for a "timely and contextual statement of faith" (37th General Council, 2000), they presented us with a lyrical gift, "something of a love song, an offering up of those values, ideas, and truths that the United Church holds close to its heart."[1]

In the material that follows, you will find that each week of Lent introduces a different "song," with gifted writers sharing their faith as they reflect on those songs. We hope you find their thoughts nourish you and challenge you, whether you read in solitude or use the resources at the back of this book for group discussion.

The ancient psalmist declares, "I will sing a new song to you, O God."(Psalm 144:9) We hope that *Singing a Song of Faith* enables you to think about your faith in new ways.

God is Holy Mystery,
beyond complete knowledge,
above perfect description…

Grateful for God's loving action,
we cannot keep from singing.

Nancy E. Hardy

---

[1] "A Song of Faith" Appendix B, available on the website of The United Church of Canada, www.united-church.ca

A SONG OF FAITH *The Refrain*

God is Holy Mystery,
beyond complete knowledge,
above perfect description.

Yet,
in love,
the one eternal God seeks relationship.

So God creates the universe
   and with it the possibility of being and relating.
God tends the universe,
   mending the broken and reconciling the estranged.
God enlivens the universe,
   guiding all things toward harmony with their Source.

Grateful for God's loving action,
we cannot keep from singing.

With the church through the ages,
we speak of God as one and triune:
Father, Son, and Holy Spirit.
We also speak of God as
   Creator, Redeemer, and Sustainer
   God, Christ, and Spirit
   Mother, Friend, and Comforter
   Source of Life, Living Word, and Bond of Love,
   and in other ways that speak faithfully of
the One on whom our hearts rely,
the fully shared life at the heart of the universe.

We witness to Holy Mystery that is Wholly Love.

God is creative and self-giving,
  generously moving
  in all the near and distant corners of the universe.
Nothing exists that does not find its source in God.
Our first response to God's providence is gratitude.
We sing thanksgiving.

WEEK ONE *We Sing of God the Creator*

Finding ourselves in a world of beauty and mystery,
   of living things, diverse and interdependent,
   of complex patterns of growth and evolution,
   of subatomic particles and cosmic swirls,
we sing of God the Creator,
the Maker and Source of all that is.

Each part of creation reveals unique aspects of God the Creator,
   who is both in creation and beyond it.
All parts of creation, animate and inanimate, are related.
All creation is good.
We sing of the Creator,
   who made humans to live and move
   and have their being in God.
In and with God,
   we can direct our lives toward right relationship
   with each other and with God.
We can discover our place as one strand in the web of life.
We can grow in wisdom and compassion.
We can recognize all people as kin.
We can accept our mortality and finitude, not as a curse,
   but as a challenge to make our lives and choices matter.

From Repentance to Renewal

Yet even now, says the Lord, return to me with all your heart.
Joel 2:12

It's Ash Wednesday, and I prepare to go to worship, hoping to meet the Holy in the mundane. For what could be more mundane than ashes—wispy reminders of their former glory, leftovers from a welcoming fireplace, dregs of life giving warmth? I enter the worship space and I am greeted by grey and silence. And I am reminded that this is a night, first of all, for repentance.

Repentance because I have been made in God's image by a Creator who made the world good and makes all things new. And I have forgotten that being part of God's complex creation means that I have responsibilities to care for the gifts of flowers and friendships. And so I read the solemn psalm: "Create in me a clean heart, O God, and put a new and right spirit within me" (Psalm 51), and listen to the call of Joel (2:12), and pray for forgiveness.

I wait in line for the ashes. Sometimes they have been mixed with refreshing waters from the baptismal font, and sometimes they're mixed with fragrant anointing oil. And sometimes, as tonight, they are left without moisture, and the grey fragments drift down my face.

Suddenly, inexplicably, I think of my mother and father, who loved to work in their garden. I remember how they saved the ashes from the wood stove all winter so they could enrich the soil in the springtime. The tone of the service changes, and we are reminded that ashes become symbols of the new life possible for us as we repent and want to change. Ashes of repentance become ashes of renewal, *"In and with God, we can direct our lives toward right relationship with each other and with God."*

With Ash Wednesday, we begin the season of Lent, when we think about Jesus as he sets his face to Jerusalem and as we reflect on his dying and rising. And of the Garden that invites us in on Easter morning.

Hymn: "Sunday's Palms Are Wednesday's Ashes" (*Voices United* 107)

Prayer: Faithful God, we bring to you the dusty ashes of our lives.
Take our burnt out dreams,
Our smouldering ambitions,
Our charred and broken promises.
Renew our spirits, and
Grant us newness of life
Through the life, death, and resurrection of Jesus Christ.
Amen.

To Think About: What are some of the "ashes" in your life? What are your hopes for this Lenten season?

Nancy E. Hardy

CONNECTING WITH GOD'S CREATION

The whole creation has been groaning in labour pain until now.
Romans 8:18-24

As I reflect on the gift of creation this evening, the unfortunate inappropriateness of my location dawns on me: a basement office at the Savannah College of Art and Design. The room is windowless and, tonight, poorly cooled with minimal puffs of conditioned air feeling more like my dog's steamy breath panting in my ear. My once nicely-pressed shirt now looks like a damp rag and probably smells only slightly better. No wonder they still wear sear-sucker in the South!

Lately, I have been troubled by the disconnection between my day-to-day experience and the natural world. Both my body and soul are out of sync with the fullness of God's creation. I leave my house and its two central air systems (one for each floor) by way of our attached garage. I slip into my air-conditioned car and, windows up, tune out the brackish smells of the marshes and muddy rivers I cross on my way downtown. When I came into my office this morning, the sun was blazing. When I leave tonight, it will be dark. My eyes will wonder how they missed the transition. My soul will stew in silence, another sunset missed.

But every now and then, God's creation asserts itself. A mighty wind blows in off the coast, washing my family and me in sheets of tropical rain. Bathed in grace, full immersion, we stop what we are doing and count the seconds between flashes of lightning and the thunder's booming shotgun blasts. We "ooh" and "ah" at the mystery of God's creation as playfully as children at a fireworks display. We hunker down, wonderfully immobilized by this force that has swept across the face of the earth for millions of years, shaping the world and breathing life into it. I sigh a wordless prayer of thanks.

HYMN: "Morning Has Broken" (*Voices United* 409)

PRAYER: Mighty God, you breathed life into the universe and you continue to breathe life into us. Open not only our five senses to your creation, but also our hearts to the beauty and our souls to the mystery of all living things connected by your eternal love. Thank you for the times we "ooh" and "ah" at sunrises and sunsets, tropical storms, or a hovering hummingbird nursing on the flower of a trumpet vine. Help us walk carefully as new beings and proper stewards in this world. Amen.

TO THINK ABOUT: In what ways have you been connected or disconnected to God's creation? How has the creation asserted itself in your life lately?

R. MARK GIULIANO

THE BODY BEAUTIFUL

God saw everything that God had made, and indeed, it was very good.
Genesis 1:26-31

I've visited many people in continuing care centres who suffer from Alzheimer's disease and whose rooms bear the same identifying marks: sparse furnishings, multiple labels, names written in capitals under smiling faces dangling from cardboard family trees. One room, however, was entirely different from those I had grown accustomed to. Above Margaret's bed hung a huge canvas: a portrait of her painted about 70 years earlier. The painting was in oil, and Margaret was in the buff—nude. Nipples, pubic hair, the whole nine yards or, more accurately, five and a half feet. There were others pictures, too...of a younger Margaret wearing bikinis.

I must have been gawking, because the parishioner I was actually visiting launched into an explanation. "Oh, you see my roommate's pictures," she said. "The family's not too happy with her, but she insists.... We all hate that painting," she added.

Why was that painting so important to Margaret? Was it because it reminded her of other seasons in life? Was it because she wanted to be certain that when people passed by they saw she was more than the near skeleton she had become? Clearly, some people found the nudity hard to live with.

Christianity has also found the body hard to live with, to varying degrees. Traditional Christian theology has proclaimed the body a thing to be shed, to get rid of, to slough off at the end of life in order to free the soul. Yet if we say, "We are created in the image of God. *All creation is good,*" how can we regard the body as a necessary evil? Why not affirm it and all its incredible functions as a blessed tool in which to *"live and move and have [our] being in God"*? Embracing a theology of embodiment doesn't mean hanging nude portraits of ourselves, but I think it does mean being a little less squeamish and judgmental of those who are unapologetically at home in their own skin.

As I was leaving, I went over to Margaret's bed, knelt down, and whispered, "I love the painting. You're beautiful." I'm not sure if she was sleeping or no longer responsive, but I like to think she heard.

HYMN: "God Who Gives to Life Its Goodness" (*Voices United* 260)

PRAYER: Wonderful God, you created us in your own image and called your creation good. As we ponder your mystery and your loving intentions for us, help us value what you've given us. Help us reflect your love by the way we live. Amen.

TO THINK ABOUT: How does the belief that we are created in the image of God challenge our negative self-perceptions?

TRISHA ELLIOTT

GIVING THANKS FOR OPPORTUNITY

I came that they may have life, and have it abundantly.
John 10:10

One of the things that I have come to appreciate most in life is that it is neither always "good" nor always "bad." Sometimes, we may catch ourselves thinking of what life would be like if things were "simpler" for us. Occasionally, while being caught up in the moment, we may even wish severe hardships on others. Yet, thankfully, life is not pure happiness or pure sorrow for anyone. There is a certain duality in all our lives.

But, at the same time, one could argue that all of life's experiences are "good"; by taking all that we are handed and learning from it, we can find something positive in everything. It is because of this that I am hesitant to place life into two broad categories. All of life can be positive.

While taking all of life's highs and lows and using them as learning experiences is not a new philosophy, I find that life has new meaning for me, especially lately.

Recently, at the end of a very long and intense day, I sat down with a group of friends. A number of different events that day had filled some of us with both happiness and sorrow, with contentment as well as guilt. Eventually, we all came together and we talked about what we had been through. Quite a number of us had felt some very strong, even negative emotions. Yet, as we continued to talk, I felt as though these emotions and the day's experiences were not "bad." Sure, some of what had happened were not the most welcome events of our lives, but I believe that the experiences had served a purpose—from unease and guilt came new understanding.

This section of "A Song of Faith" about God the Creator touches on how all things are related and how we should give our thanks to the Creator for all the opportunities presented to us. Our actions impact not only ourselves, but others as well. These "good" and "bad" experiences shape who we really are. And for that, I can be truly thankful to God.

HYMN: "God Is the One Whom We Seek Together" (*Voices United* 283)

PRAYER: Creator God, we give you thanks for the times we are able to think and talk about what is good in life. We give you thanks that we are part of you and one another. Help us grow in understanding of what you would have us do. Amen.

TO THINK ABOUT: Think of times in which something negative happened and look for as many positives as you can from this experience.

ROBERT PIKE

WEEK TWO *We Sing of Grace*

*M*ade in the image of God,
we yearn for the fulfillment that is life in God.
Yet we choose to turn away from God.
We surrender ourselves to sin,
  a disposition revealed in selfishness, cowardice, or apathy.
Becoming bound and complacent
  in a web of false desires and wrong choices,
  we bring harm to ourselves and others.
This brokenness in human life and community
  is an outcome of sin.
Sin is not only personal
  but accumulates
  to become habitual and systemic forms
  of injustice, violence, and hatred.

We are all touched by this brokenness:
  the rise of selfish individualism
    that erodes human solidarity;
  the concentration of wealth and power
    without regard for the needs of all;
  the toxins of religious and ethnic bigotry;
  the degradation of the blessedness of human bodies
    and human passions through sexual exploitation;
  the delusion of unchecked progress and limitless growth
  that threatens our home, the earth;
  the covert despair that lulls many into numb complicity
  with empires and systems of domination.
We sing lament and repentance.

Yet evil does not—cannot—
  undermine or overcome the love of God.
God forgives,
  and calls all of us to confess our fears and failings
  with honesty and humility.
God reconciles,
  and calls us to repent the part we have played

in damaging our world, ourselves, and each other.
God transforms,
    and calls us to protect the vulnerable,
    to pray for deliverance from evil,
    to work with God for the healing of the world,
    that all might have abundant life.
We sing of grace.

Sunday Refrain: Lament Transformed

God is Holy Mystery,
beyond complete knowledge,
above perfect description.

Yet…

God tends the universe,
mending the broken and reconciling the estranged.[2]

"We must be getting close to Lent," sighed one of my choir members. "We're starting to practise all that sad music. I hate it!"

I tried to explain that Lent wasn't just about sad music, but was a quiet time—a time of reflection, a period of time set aside in the church for going more deeply into ourselves as we think about Jesus and his journey to Jerusalem. I may have convinced myself, but I could tell that she wasn't buying my explanation. For her, Lent was a time when we sang sad songs.

But, of course, sad songs are part of it, aren't they? Traditionally, the church has suggested a threefold form of discipline for Lent: prayer, for the good of our souls; fasting, for the good of our bodies; and almsgiving, for the good of our neighbours. We begin Lent with Ash Wednesday and a call to repentance and we are reminded that we're part of a world that is not all God intended it to be. We are part of a world where there is violence, oppression, suffering. We are part of systems that despoil the earth and perpetuate poverty. Sad songs are appropriate; we need to sing lament and repentance.

---

[2] The full refrain from "A Song of Faith" appears on page 11.

But even as we lament, we are aware that *"God tends the universe, mending the broken and reconciling the estranged."* We know about courage and singing as African grandmothers care for children whose parents have died of AIDS; we see flowers pushing through the asphalt of shopping mall parking lots that once were fertile fields; we find hope in people of all ages who refuse to give in to disappointment and apathy while they work for change.

God's compassion transforms our laments to songs of grace.

HYMN: "We Cannot Measure How You Heal" (*Voices United* 613)

PRAYER: O God, we thank you for hearing our songs of lament
and confession.
Thank you for your note of mercy.
Forgive us when we hurt, rather than heal,
and help us walk in your way, as Jesus did,
with his face turned to Jerusalem. Amen.

TO THINK ABOUT: What is it about your personal life or the world that causes you to lament? Where do you see signs of God's grace?

NANCY E. HARDY

FREEING US FROM BONDAGE

The Lord heard our voice and saw our affliction, our toil, and our oppression.
Deuteronomy 26:1-11

"A wandering Aramean, I," sang the preacher when he wanted to draw his congregation into his tale. "It may sound like I'm telling an old, old story," he added, "but this is my story and yours." The story he had in mind did come from long, long ago. It was of the descent of their people into Egypt; it was the story of the human race. In Egypt they multiplied, but found themselves shut out of life. They fell victim to ethnic bigotry and surrendered to a degraded existence. Broken and disregarded, they found themselves bound in a system of domination.

We understand how hard it is to get back to being children of God, creatures in the image of the Creator. We know it's not the little things we do from time to time, but deep-rooted self-interest that cuts us off from the Creator and robs us of life. Will we never be free? Through long experience we've learned we can't do it on our own.

Some days it felt as though they'd never find fulfillment. How often they'd sat around at night thinking up new schemes for escape! Nothing ever came of them. At their lowest point, they admitted they were powerless to free themselves. They sang lament.

But they were not alone. The Holy One heard their voice and their oppression—hears our voice, our oppression, and acts to meet our yearning for real life, the good life. God is determined to see a breakthrough, to draw us towards the light and give us rebirth. Simply put, this is Creator's business, to make the creature fully alive. "That's the old and oft repeated story," said the preacher. "So let's sing that chorus again, and this time, sing it like we really mean it. 'A wandering Aramean, I....'"

HYMN: "Lead On, O Cloud of Presence" (*Voices United* 421)

PRAYER: God of all ages,
 Thank you for your faithfulness
  and your persistence in the face of our continuing rebellion
  and self-centredness.
 Be with us on our journey to wholeness;
 grant us an awareness of your loving presence
  and help us see your light. Amen.

TO THINK ABOUT: From what is God working to liberate us today? How does God free us?

V. MARTYN SADLER

GRACE UNLIMITED

"...consider whether the light in you is not darkness."
Luke 11:33-36

On the way to an urban outreach centre, I walked past her sitting on the curb. She caught my eye and held it. I looked at her for a minute, then turned away and rounded the corner into the centre where I was meeting the director. She was giving me a ride to her home for an end-of-year party.

When we emerged from the centre, the director gasped. "What happened?" she asked the woman on the curb, running up, kneeling down. "I twisted my ankle and fell. I tried to get up, but I can't," came the weak reply.

It turned out that the woman I'd passed by was a Board member I had never met, but who was invited to the party too. My embarrassment rose as I helped lift her into the front seat of the car. I wanted to explain that I thought she was a street person. I wanted to ask, "Why didn't you tell me that you needed help?" I wanted to defend myself—to make lousy excuses, to shift the blame. But I had nothing good to say in my defence, so I fumbled an apology and crawled into the backseat with my shame.

I had become so complacent, so accustomed to poverty, so ignorant of it that I failed to question it, to inquire. *"Sin is not only personal but accumulates to become habitual and systemic forms of injustice...."* I had made two unnerving assumptions: that this woman was a street person and that as such I had nothing to offer her. In the instant it took to walk by, my grace was exposed for what it was—limited. Mine was grace upon demand. Christ's is grace before and beyond demand.

I would have given anything in that naked moment to crawl away and hide. However, from the backseat, from a place of shame, the Spirit visited grace upon my embarrassment. The Spirit blessed me with a painful "blind, but now I see" moment—the insight and desire to live a more forgiving, grace-filled life.

Hymn: "Will You Come and Follow Me?" (*Voices United* 567)

Prayer: Amazing God, how can it be that in spite of my arrogance, my complacency, my shame, you should care for me and shower me with your endless mercy? Thank you! Help me be more attentive and walk in your way. Amen.

To Think About: When have I been guilty of a sin of omission or sin of commission? What's the difference between the two?

Trisha Elliott

SMALL WAVES ADD UP TO TIDES

The days are surely coming, says the Lord, when I will make a new covenant...they shall all know me, from the least of them to the greatest, says the Lord; for I will forgive their iniquity and remember their sin no more.
Jeremiah 31:31-34

Sin is something with which everyone must grapple; it is not restricted by anything. Sin is a part of who we are, despite how hard we may try to argue that it is not. So how do we deal with sin on a personal level? Often we will suppress it, or put a stop to it. We may change our actions for the better. These steps are adequate for easily identifiable forms of sin, but what happens when we are ignorant, or complacent, in our sinning?

Let me explain. Within an increasingly technologically connected world, personal connections are beginning to fade. At one point, news of a tragic fire and the lives it claimed would have brought communities together to pray, to offer help. It still does, but not to the extent it once did. Now, within communities, especially in the larger cities, there is a growing apathy toward suffering. From fires in communities to genocides in other nations, our society seems willing to shrug it off, saying "That's life."

But as Christians, we are called to be conscious of what we can do to change things for the better. Sometimes, it may seem as though any effort on our part would be so miniscule compared with the amount of effort it would take to change things, that we would be wasting our time. But whenever I think that way, a certain passage from Charles Mackay's *The Old and the New* comes to mind. Mackay uses water as an excellent analogy. He points out that the slightest wave on the ocean's surface may eventually form part of the tide, and sometimes by sheer numbers of smaller waves, larger waves are formed.

Timing also plays a part. If we stay conscious of what we must do and contribute our efforts collectively, we can, through the guidance of God, make a difference in this world of ours.

Hymn: "What Does the Lord Require of You?" (*Voices United* 701)

Prayer: O God, make us instruments of your peace. Where there is hardship in our communities, call us together to bring help to the suffering. Give us hope that no matter how small our actions may be, we can still make a difference. Pour your mercy on our sins. Amen.

To Think About: What kind of suffering goes on in your community? What steps can you take to help the situation become better?

Robert Pike

GRACE WAKES US UP

Encourage one another and build up each other.
1 Thessalonians 5:6-11

(God) will neither slumber nor sleep.
Psalm 121

When I first arrived in Savannah, an older colleague warned me that Southerners love you to hammer them with sin. He said, "If you preached nothing but guilt for sin, you'd pack the place every Sunday." But having been raised and trained in The United Church of Canada and now serving in a denomination that's equally liberal, I just can't bring myself to do it.

At the same time, I realize we have to take sin seriously. After all, if it weren't real or if it didn't have a destructively dark power in our lives and in the world, then we wouldn't need God's grace at all. Sin is that which separates us from God and from each other. Grace brings us back. Sin is the thinking, or action, or lack thereof that muddies the image of God within us. Grace washes us clean.

I'm not sure which is the biggest of our sins: *"selfish individualism," "religious and ethnic bigotry,"* or any of the others found in "A Song of Faith." But it seems to me one of the most dangerous is our own *"numb complicity"* in sin, our denial of it, especially in the church. Too often, that denial of sin within the church ruins good ministries and good people. We forget that sin has no better hiding place than within the church and, sadly, we too often behave accordingly.

In this context, I would recommend your reading Canadian author Douglas Coupland's pre-millennial, apocalyptic novel *Girlfriend in a Coma*.[3] In Coupland's book, the world doesn't meet its demise by some nuclear or biological catastrophe, but by people who fall asleep and allow the world to spin into chaos.

Grace keeps waking us up to our sin. Grace also wakes us up to a new and faithful way of being in the world.

HYMN: "Sleepers, Wake" (*Voices United* 711)

PRAYER: Gracious God, who neither sleeps nor slumbers, you watch over us by day and by night, you guard us with strength and preserve our dignity during times of trouble, and you celebrate with us in times of joy. You break in on our lives, O God, like a thief in the night and you bring to us grace and truth. We ask that you keep us awake to your abiding presence. Help us stand watch to the ways we muddy your image within us and to the ways that your coming grace washes us clean again. Restore within us a clean heart and new spirit that we might live as new beings in this old world. Amen.

TO THINK ABOUT: How do we deny the sin in our church and our lives? How do we experience God's grace in those situations?

R. MARK GIULIANO

---

[3] Douglas Coupland *Girlfriend in a Coma* (Regan Books, 1999).

FINDING GOD'S FORGIVENESS

We have peace with God through our Lord Jesus Christ, through whom we have obtained access to this grace in which we stand.
Romans 5:1-5

When I was growing up, sin was mainly equated with sex, premarital or extramarital (always assuming that stealing, lying, and murder also fell into that category). Then as a society, we moved on. "Sin" became an old-fashioned, outmoded, and definitely "not ok" word. United Church people began to say that, really, the prayer of confession was meaningless, even offensive. And sometimes it probably was, given the way the prayer was often worded.

Still, regardless of changing attitudes, it would be a great loss, I think, to toss out such solid ancient concepts as "sin" and its opposite, "righteousness," which means enjoying right and just relationships with family, co-workers, friends, our fellow creatures, the planet, and with God. In our hearts we know how often we don't get it right. And, in spite of all the compelling reasons why we get it wrong (our temperament, upbringing, unhappy circumstances, our need to survive and assert ourselves....), we also know that we have at least a small degree of choice—and so responsibility and accountability. Guilt, like love, is elemental.

It is also communal. The night air at our cottage used to be filled with a cacophony of bullfrog noise. Then one year it went silent. The bullfrogs were gone. This past summer, our land was devastated by a tornado and the public beaches were closed more often than before. "It's the heat," they said, "and it will probably get worse." Small things perhaps compared with drought or a vanishing water supply. But when I think of our misuse and greedy gobbling up of the earth's resources I feel awash in guilt.

Individually and corporately we so much need God's forgiveness. We need God's grace to effect change and give us the hope that, together, we can realize abundant life for ourselves and all of creation.

HYMN: "There's a Wideness in God's Mercy" (*Voices United* 271)

PRAYER: Holy God: without wanting to, many of us are dragging behind a large bag of regrets and sorrow for all those things we have done and all those things we have left undone. You realize, even more than we do, our self-absorption and the meagreness of compassion, our indifference to what is happening in the larger human family and to the earth. Forgive us, gracious God. Give us your grace. Piece together our brokenness, so that we and our world may be made whole.

TO THINK ABOUT: When do you feel yourself most in need of God's forgiveness and grace?

PATRICIA WELLS

COMMUNION BLESSINGS

Each of us was given grace according to the measure of Christ's gift.
Ephesians 4:7

For some reason I've had communion on my mind. Maybe it's because it's Lent, everything now moving inexorably toward that moment when Jesus breaks bread with his friends for the last time.

I've been part of the re-enactment of that ritual a thousand times: huddled around a smoky woodstove in a cabin with a little group of friends, passing the bread from hand to hand; lining up with hundreds in a huge arena to dip the bread in a cup of wine and circle around to (hopefully) the same seat I started in; sitting in the choir at my own church, trying to balance the little silver tray and sing at the same time; sitting in a pew; gathered around a table; standing in a big tent; clustered in a chapel.

And I wonder why I do it. I know I get uneasy if I think I might be left out. (Will they remember the choir? Are the reporters at this event—of which I am one—invited to take part? Once I slipped up to Archbishop Desmond Tutu to take his photo as he served communion, and then paused anxiously. He winked at me and held out the bread.)

It may be that my hunger for the bread and wine is actually explained here, in this passage from "A Song of Faith." Because, as it says, I am often broken, I make wrong choices, I taste the despair that North American affluence hides too well.

But this bread is about grace. This bread gives me the hope of change. And so, over and over again, I form a circle with my friends and say the words: "The bread of new life…the cup of blessing." I reach out for these things for which I yearn, and I am given them—just at it says here, in this song: Forgiveness. Reconciliation. Abundant life. Transformation.

That's why I take communion.

HYMN: "Eat This Bread and Never Hunger" (*Voices United* 471)

A PRAYER FOR GRACE:
  God of abundant life
  Grant us grace.
  God of reconciliation
  Grant us grace.
  God of forgiveness
  Grant us grace.
  In the name of Jesus,
   who holds the bread out to us,
  Transform us. Amen.

TO THINK ABOUT: Do you experience God's grace in communion? How does it happen?

DONNA SINCLAIR

WEEK THREE *We Sing of God the Spirit*

The fullness of life includes
  moments of unexpected inspiration and courage lived out,
  experiences of beauty, truth, and goodness,
  blessings of seeds and harvest,
    friendship and family, intellect and sexuality,
  the reconciliation of persons through justice
    and communities living in righteousness,
    and the articulation of meaning.
And so we sing of God the Spirit,
  who from the beginning has swept over the face of creation,
  animating all energy and matter
  and moving in the human heart.

We sing of God the Spirit,
  faithful and untameable,
  who is creatively and redemptively active in the world.

The Spirit challenges us to celebrate the holy
  not only in what is familiar,
  but also in that which seems foreign.

We sing of the Spirit,
  who speaks our prayers of deepest longing
  and enfolds our concerns and confessions,
  transforming us and the world.

SUNDAY REFRAIN: THE SPIRIT RETURNS

God is Holy Mystery,
beyond complete knowledge,
above perfect description.

Yet...
God enlivens the universe,
guiding all things toward harmony with their Source.[4]

During the late sixties, when I was in ministry in a church in Fredericton, I received an invitation to attend the annual meeting of the Canadian Council of Churches. I was thrilled to be invited and went filled with a spirit of excitement and enthusiasm.

It wasn't long before I discovered that large church meetings are about the same as any other meeting. We suffered through the same procedural wrangles, the same competing groups, the same exhaustion from long days of debates. My spirit of excitement soon evaporated.

But one evening was different. It had been a long day—the meeting had been angry and bitter, and we finally quit because people were too tired to sit anymore. Little groups sat and talked while the leaders planned strategy. Then I spied a piano in the corner, and a friend and I went over and started to sing.

At first, there were angry glares from people whose important conversations we were interrupting, but gradually, others drifted over to join us. We sang for hours. We sang Welsh hymns and gospel hymns, old songs and new songs, and by the end of the evening, everyone was singing. The hostility and tension disappeared, and we finally joined hands and finished with

---

[4] The full refrain from "A Song of Faith" appears on page 11.

"We Shall Overcome." It was a wonderful moment; I knew the Spirit had returned. And the next day, we were able to continue our meetings with renewed energy.

The Gospel of Luke tells us that when Jesus was beginning his ministry, the Spirit led him into the desert. (Luke 4:1) For a time, while he wrestled with his demons, it seemed that the Spirit had disappeared. But in the end, Jesus knew he was not alone, and the Spirit would continue to be with him while he carried out his mission.

The Bible tells us that the Spirit was present in the chaos of creation, in the despair of exile, and the wilderness of abandonment. The Spirit is with us in our desert times, holding us with tenderness and encouraging us to go out into the world.

HYMN: "There's a Spirit in the Air" (*Voices United* 582)

PRAYER: Spirit God,
>Who speaks our prayers for us
>>with sighs too deep for words,
>Hold us in your love
>>and comfort us with your presence,
>That we might be renewed and encouraged
>To do our part in the healing of your world. Amen.

TO THINK ABOUT: What signs of God's Spirit have you experienced in your life?

NANCY E. HARDY

GENTLE BREEZE OR HURRICANE?

And the Spirit immediately drove him out into the wilderness.
Mark 1:9-14

While on vacation a number of years ago, our family experienced a minor meltdown. We were tired and hungry, hunting aimlessly for a restaurant in a strange town, and the kids' bickering in the back seat was about to evolve into a full-scale battle of the wills. Abruptly and wisely, my wife pulled to the side of the road and ordered them out with instructions to "work it out." Dumbfounded, the kids unpacked themselves from the back of the car. Much to our surprise, while my wife and I sat quietly inside the car, our children not only worked out their differences, but in mere seconds, even worked out a route back to the hotel. We forgot that they were carrying the room key!

A favourite hymn in our congregation is James K. Manley's "Spirit, Spirit of Gentleness." Our music director, one of Savannah's exceptional nightclub pianists, really lets it flow on our little baby grand while I spiritedly strum along on my guitar. But if you've ever experienced the transforming power of God's Spirit, you know that the Spirit can be anything but "gentle." Sometimes it puts you out on the side of the road to make peace with God, with others, and with the world.

Sometimes God's Spirit breaks in on our lives, shaking our souls the way a gale force wind shakes the house and rattles the windows. Luke says that for the first church, God's Spirit blew through the walls of fear and confusion with the "rush of a violent wind" (Acts 2:2) and moved the young congregation out into city streets, empowered with a new voice for the dangerous proclamation of the gospel. Mark says that after Jesus' baptism, the Holy Spirit "drove" him out into the lonely wilderness (Mark 1:12) to clarify both his identity and his mission.

When I look back on my life, it was often the violent winds that drove me out of my safe places and into deeper and clearer relationship with God. Some Sunday, instead of "Spirit, Spirit of Gentleness," I'd like to sing Neil Young's "You Are Like a Hurricane."

HYMN: "Spirit, Spirit of Gentleness" (*Voices United* 375)
or "Like a Hurricane" (© 1976, 1977, Silver Fiddle)

PRAYER: Mighty God, whose Spirit, like the wind, blows where
it wants, shaping and transforming our lives, you
drove the fearful disciples into the world with the bold
proclamation of your good news. So, too, move us beyond
our self-centred anxieties that we might reach out and
reach others. Help us hoist a sail and catch the breeze you
send our way. Teach us to trust your Spirit not only when
it lifts us, but also when it roars into our lives taking us in
new directions.

To THINK ABOUT: Is the Spirit a gentle breeze or a hurricane that pushes you out of your safe places into a deeper relationship with God and the world?

R. MARK GIULIANO

THE SPIRIT BREATHES LIFE

*O Lord, you have searched me and known me.... Where can
I go from your Spirit?*
Psalm 139:1-12

It often seems curious that at a time when spirituality is so much in fashion, the Spirit is so ignored. Let me explain what I mean…

These days, the word "spirituality" is ubiquitous. Typically, in the last book I read on nutrition there was a section on meditation. Meditation, along with exercise, was said to be critical in maintaining good health. Now I don't for a moment dispute the fact that meditation changes both body chemistry and brain waves for the better, or that the sweet peacefulness that comes with such relaxation is good in itself. As a Christian, however, I'd like to ask, "But why stop there? Why not consciously include the Spirit in our search for spiritual well-being?"

In traditional Christian mysticism, clearing of the mind was often seen as a prelude to opening oneself to the Holy Spirit, like a plant turning to the light. An early Celtic prayer speaks of resting with the Spirit in her "sun garden of love." It calls you to imagine sitting with your back against a sun-warmed garden wall, surrounded by golden light, the fragrance of growing things, and presence of the Spirit. That might lead into spoken prayer, but not necessarily. In itself, it is enough.

I think the whole depth and breadth of the Spirit's work is also frequently overlooked within the church by those who see its activity as basically saving individual souls and maintaining a conventional public morality. That assumption may be comfortable, but it isn't biblical. In the Bible, the Spirit breathes life into every good action and every movement toward social wholeness. Biblical spirituality, through prophets, judges, kings, to Jesus and the early church, has a tough political grittiness.

The Spirit, who moved over the waters of creation, blows where, when, how, and in whom she wishes.

HYMN: "In the Quiet Curve of Evening" (*Voices United* 278)

PRAYER: Holy Spirit, you who breathe life into the most distant star and every atom of our being, we open ourselves to you, asking that you would fill us to overflowing with your presence. In stillness and silence, envelop us with your peace. Then blow through us, urging us to life with holy greed and to a goodness only you can imagine.

TO THINK ABOUT: What difference can the work of the Spirit make to our lives and the life of the world?

PATRICIA WELLS

UNEXPECTED BEAUTY AND PROMISE

Suddenly...a sound like the rush of a violent wind.
Acts 2:1-4

I couldn't believe what I was seeing. I had to blink. Several times.

Paintings were everywhere: on the back of cans, on blue striped sheets, on cardboard box covers; tacked up on the walls, the ceiling, even the floor. I couldn't move and didn't know where to look first. It was like standing in 10 art galleries at once. It was the closest I've ever come to being dazzled.

Karen, the artist, suffered from schizophrenia. That fact I knew before I paid her (and she me) an unforgettable pastoral visit. What I didn't know was that Karen was also an artistic genius—a genius who, I would later learn, had been discovered by several gallery owners. While in bad times Karen's illness drove her to live on the street or sleep on her mother's couch and in good times find shelter in her own rent-geared-to-income apartment, her art was being housed, shown, and admired in some of the most glamorous galleries in the city.

Standing in Karen's living room that morning was like standing in the heart of the Holy Spirit. It was wild. It was uninhibited. It was unimaginably beautiful.

There are times when the Holy Spirit enters our lives and knocks us off our feet, sweeping us to situations, places, and people we never thought we'd draw near. While it's comforting to think of a Spirit who soothes and calms, the Bible also tells us that the Spirit upsets, tears down, flies, and burns. God's untameable Spirit was evident in the Red Sea, in the Jordan, on the Emmaus road...and in Karen's astounding apartment.

I doubt my visit had much of an impact on Karen, but I will never forget the impact it had on me. God's creative Spirit at work in Karen blew me away. Since then I've discovered that Spirit moments are like that. Lifting. Levelling. And the Spirit of God is like that. She enters brokenness and pain and plasters life with unexpected beauty and promise.

HYMN: "With the Wings of Our Mind" (*Voices United* 698)

PRAYER: Wild and unfathomable God, let me feel the wings of your Spirit, that I might dance and sing and delight in your hovering. Help me break free and live in your beauty and promise. Amen.

TO THINK ABOUT: Have you ever experienced the Spirit in brokenness and pain? When has the Spirit touched your heart unexpectedly?

TRISHA ELLIOTT

The Spirit Is Here

In the beginning…the Spirit of God swept over the face of the waters.
Genesis 1:1-2

I'm writing this in autumn. You'll be reading this in early spring. The light is changing, slanting golden across the backyard, falling to dark earlier. The colours are shifting with the lessening of light, the green deserting the maple leaves to make way for scarlet.

I gather seeds. I'll be planting them in spring when you are reading this, ferreting out the seed trays I put away in entirely the wrong place, so that I have to dig through four feet of snow into the backyard shed to find them.

I rove the garden storing up beauty, plotting the wonders to come. I make brutal and arbitrary choices about which plants must go (that poppy, too orange; those sundrops, too weedy). I'll dig them out come spring and divide the daylilies, so as to have little, singing, golden yellow trumpets everywhere.

They say we are bereft of meaning now, the old ways slipping, the ancient religions suspect and ignored. But they are wrong. The Spirit is here, and this work of my hands is the very *"articulation of meaning"* this "Song of Faith" proclaims.

Yes, God is here, and Hallelujah for it. Autumn, winter, spring, and summer, the *"blessings of seeds and harvest,"* yes. Eli my grandson will make angels in the snow, and leave. In the blink of an eye, he'll come back again from far away and we'll plant pumpkins, tucking the large flat seeds into a mound of dirt.

The seasons tumble past.

In the spring, when you are reading this, the first small green shoots of crocus will be bursting out of the ground. Soon after that, perfect strangers will pause and ask about that vine that covers the house, and teenage boys will say "nice garden" out of the corner of their mouths as they fly by on skateboards. I will lean on my shovel, humming, because the Spirit is sweeping over the face of creation, moving in every human heart, transforming our world.

HYMN: "Spirit Dancing" (*Voices United* 388)

A PRAYER OF GRATITUDE:
> God the Spirit
> Who sweeps over the face of Creation
> We celebrate your beauty.
> God the Spirit
> Who sweeps through our hearts like wind
> We celebrate your love.
> Hallelujah for it all.
> Amen.

TO THINK ABOUT: What signs of God's Spirit give you hope for creation?

DONNA SINCLAIR

RESTORING HOPE

To set the mind on the Spirit is life and peace.
Romans 8:6*b*

*"The fullness of life includes moments of unexpected
inspiration...."* ("A Song of Faith")

This passage, like the others before it, touches on how vast and
beautiful creation is. It is not the only theme that is contained within,
but it is the one I would like to mention.

When we think of the complexity and yet the sheer simplicity of our
world, how can we not know that there is a higher power at work?
Someone once said that humanity is the by-product of a few natural laws,
and that any change in those constants could remove us from the universe.
Humanity's existence is a strange coincidence. While I do not know
enough to effectively argue with the first point, I find myself slightly at
odds with the second statement.

Last spring, I had the opportunity to go on an interior camping and
canoe trip in Algonquin Park (in Ontario). Algonquin Park might not be
the most remote and uncharted locale on earth, but as we were travelling
through some particularly winding rivers, a sense of solitude and serenity
set in. I do not know if it was the mist, or the warmth of my breath
clouding up my glasses, but it became very quiet as a light fog set in.
Eventually, as the sun started to pierce the clouds overhead, we broke free
of the winding river and came upon a beautiful lake. I remember that,
sometime later, it occurred to me how truly beautiful it was to be drifting
slowly in the midst of this large body of water with only the distant calls of
loons and the hushed chattering of my companions to break an otherwise
blanketing silence.

It was, as my philosophy teacher tried to explain to some disinterested students last year, a moment of aesthetic pleasure. In this moment of pure sensation, I could see the validity of certain aspects of the theory of Intelligent Design. What could create such beauty that it would leave me in such awe? I'm not so sure about it being chance; what I saw was too moving to be explained away by probabilities and coincidences.

HYMN: "Many and Great, O God, Are Your Works" (*Voices United* 308)

PRAYER: Spirit God, we find you in many places, especially in those of natural beauty and silence. Thank you for northern lakes, shimmering birch trees, and the cry of the loon. Thank you for moments of unexpected beauty when we sense your presence. Help us remember, so we can carry those moments into our everyday living. Amen.

TO THINK ABOUT: What are some moments in your life where you may have doubted your faith, yet something simple restored your hope?

ROBERT PIKE

SPIRIT MYSTERY

If we live by the Spirit, let us also be guided by the Spirit.
Galatians 5:22-26

I'm lucky to live in a region of many artists. The older I get, the more often I find the Spirit in works of art—and the more often I try to stand beside artists in hopes that the passing Spirit will let a feather fall on me.

I see a child's excitement when he's unleashed with a crayon on a blank page, and the awe in his eyes as he picks up autumn leaves. Another child studies stones and asks me to carry them for her, my pockets bulging. I look forward to next year, hoping it will be her turn for leaves. And do you remember a time when every flower needed to be sniffed, lest a single possibility of beauty be missed? (How patient people are with children on their lawns, mining their riches.) I suspect child and artist are alive to things I don't see. The Spirit speaks to them of beauty I'm blind to.

Sure, there are times when the artist tells me something of the pain of human existence, the absence of beauty in the human condition. Those moments are harder to take. I'd rather hear the good-news stories, but I sense the artist's honesty and allow myself to be carried along to insight.

The artist, like the child, often leaves me mystified, asking, "Now where did that come from? How did those two things get pulled together?" Words can't explain it. When they try to explain, we have a treatise or a how-to column. Like form and colour, words speak intriguing ambiguity. As long as I can't say for sure, I can't possess it fully. It remains mystery, with the whir of Spirit wings overhead.

On the way home I check my shoulders for a feather.

HYMN: "She Comes Sailing on the Wind" (*Voices United* 380)

PRAYER: Mysterious God,
　　　Your Spirit dances through our lives,
　　　　swirling sounds and sights that leave us breathless.
　　　Tune our lives, that we might move with your beauty
　　　　and be open to your goodness
　　　　for our sake and the sake of others. Amen.

TO THINK ABOUT: What gifts of the Spirit does God bring into your life?

V. MARTYN SADLER

WEEK FOUR *We Sing of Scripture and Worship*

We offer worship
  as an outpouring of gratitude and awe
  and a practice of opening ourselves
  to God's still, small voice of comfort,
  to God's rushing whirlwind of challenge.
Through word, music, art, and sacrament,
  in community and in solitude,
  God changes our lives, our relationships, and our world.
We sing with trust.

Scripture is our song for the journey, the living word
  passed on from generation to generation
  to guide and inspire,
  that we might wrestle a holy revelation for our time and place
  from the human experiences
    and cultural assumptions of another era.
God calls us to be doers of the word and not hearers only.

The Spirit breathes revelatory power into scripture,
  bestowing upon it a unique and normative place
  in the life of the community.
The Spirit judges us critically when we abuse scripture
  by interpreting it narrow-mindedly,
  using it as a tool of oppression, exclusion, or hatred.

The wholeness of scripture testifies
  to the oneness and faithfulness of God.
The multiplicity of scripture testifies to its depth:
  two testaments, four gospels,
  contrasting points of view held in tension—
all a faithful witness to the One and Triune God,
the Holy Mystery that is Wholly Love.

SUNDAY REFRAIN:
THE GIFT OF SCRIPTURE

God is Holy Mystery,
beyond complete knowledge,
above perfect description…

Grateful for God's loving action,
we cannot keep from singing.[5]

For most of us there are certain sayings that sum up our approach to life: "In this world there is no free lunch," "No pain, no gain," "It's not perfect, but it will do."

If we are people of faith and know our scripture well, we probably also use Bible verses in the same way. They walk with us and help us through tough times. Isaiah has been a constant companion of mine, and this passage has lightened many an anxious moment:

"Those who wait upon the Lord shall renew their strength,
they shall mount up with wings like eagles,
they shall run and not be weary,
they shall walk and not faint." (Isaiah 40:31)

The gift of scripture, *"our song for the journey,"* is multi-faceted. I find comfort in the poetry of Isaiah; I am convicted by phrases like "mercy triumphs over judgment" (James 2:13); I am inspired by the stories and sayings of Jesus. But if there's an argument about what the Bible says about so and so, I don't pick out scripture verses like Jack Horner pulling out a plum to prove something. For me, wrestling a holy revelation for our time and place means taking the Bible seriously, but not literally.

When I was a young school teacher living in Thunder Bay, I attended a

---

[5] The full refrain from "A Song of Faith" appears on page 11.

Bible study group led by Lois Wilson, who later became the Moderator of The United Church of Canada. I'll never forget the night I discovered that the Adam and Eve story was not to be taken literally. Adam simply means "man," and Eve means "woman," said Lois. And my mind said, "So now it all makes sense! Now I understand that we can read the Bible with our minds, not just our hearts." And what a difference it has made to me!

For I began to study and discover the many layers of this "Book of Books": the history of God's covenant people; the songs of a shepherd king; the gospels of Jesus Christ; the inspiring letters from Paul and his contemporaries. Grateful for this gift, I "*cannot keep from singing.*"

HYMN: "God, Who Has Caused to Be Written" (*Voices United* 498)

PRAYER: God of wisdom and understanding,
We thank you for your Word in scripture.
It is a constant source of comfort
and a guide for our living.
Help us to read and reflect
and in our meditation
find your Spirit speaking to us,
and your love inspiring us.
We pray through Jesus, whose words became your Word.
Amen.

TO THINK ABOUT: What scripture verses have been most helpful to you? What is your favourite Bible passage or story?

NANCY E. HARDY

SPEAKING THE LANGUAGE OF LOVE

We will tell to the coming generation the glorious deeds of the Lord.
Psalm 78

Since Eli was born, I've been looking at scripture differently. Eli is my grandson's name, short for Elijah. I hold him on my knee and talk to him about his famous ancestor, the prophet Elijah, who was fed by ravens; Elijah, who outruns King Ahab's horses.

Eli looks at me with huge, dark eyes. At two months, I'm not sure he understands. Of course, I don't tell him about his famous ancestor mocking the prophets of Baal until they slash themselves "with swords and lances until the blood gushed out over them." (1 Kings 18:28) Nor do I say that he then orders Baal's prophets taken to the Wadi Kershon and killed, all 450 of them.

The dry riverbed must have run with blood. It's not a pretty picture of Elijah or his God.

And yet I love Elijah, prophet and grandson both. I love the trust with which the prophet vanishes into the wilderness on God's command, and I love those swooping ravens, bringing bread. I love his prophet ways, warning the angry king there will be drought. He speaks to me of global warming, too-rapid burning of the ancient forests gone to oil, which are the inheritance of our grandchildren.

Northrop Frye said that the Bible is the language of love, and I believe it. He said it is proclamation contained in the language of myth, and I believe that too. Myth is a universe complete in itself, of high drama and wisdom and the greatest truth. It tells me everything I need to know about my

God's faithfulness to me. But I have to go there, into it, and live each story as my own.

I have to accept Elijah's courage and reject his bloody-minded vengeance.

Eli watches me, wide-eyed. He listens to his story, as much as I will tell today. I am proud to do this. Scripture, says "A Song of Faith," is *the living word passed on from generation to generation to guide and inspire."*

HYMN: "I Love to Tell the Story" (*Voices United* 343)

A PRAYER FOR TRUTH:
>   God of prophets and kings and babies,
>   Whose faithfulness we trust,
>   Reveal to us your truth.
>   God who is found in words and music and babies,
>   We thank you for the stories
>   of Jesus and all the prophets.
>   We thank you for your truthfulness. Amen.

TO THINK ABOUT: How do we pass on our faith to our children and grandchildren?

DONNA SINCLAIR

THE BIBLE TELLS ME SO

How sweet are your words to my taste.
Psalm 119:97-11

After my husband and children, I am most passionate about the Bible. My passion stems back to the days when sleep was something I took great pains to avoid, and the Bible was the one book I was allowed to stay up and read as late as I wanted. Between grades six and seven I read the whole thing cover to cover. That was when I fell in love.

I love the Bible's weight of stories. I love that it is many things rolled into one: poetry, music, liturgy, history, mythology, fact, fiction.... I love that it frustrates, confounds, intrigues, and inspires me. I love that brilliant minds debate single lines of text and that more "ordinary" people find in its verses enough to get them through the day. I love it when people find in her passages the courage to serve others, not by loudly pounding out quotes and proof texts, but by quietly serving, because that's what Jesus did.

Do I believe that Jonah was literally swallowed by a whale? No. But I love that a storyteller somewhere, sometime told the truest of stories about how lonely, dark, and isolating life without God can be. Do I believe that Adam and Eve literally stood in a paradise called Eden? I doubt it. But I know the story's warning about temptation is true because I've stood outside Eden. Am I surprised that the Bible occasionally reflects unpalatable aspects of its time and culture? No. Frankly, I'm amazed that it doesn't reflect its time and culture more often. And it doesn't stop making me a believer.

I love the power the 23rd Psalm has to comfort broken spirits. I love how "Our Father who art in heaven" unites and so often offers closure to our deepest prayers. I love how the Song of Solomon makes sex sacred and how the Beatitudes promise a brighter day. I love the rainbow, the burning bush, the mustard seed, and the empty cross. But mostly I love that while

I've spent 20 of my 32 years loving the Bible, and the last 15 earnestly studying it, I will still spend the rest of my life getting to know it.

HYMN: "God, Whose Almighty Word" (*Voices United* 313)

PRAYER: God of wisdom, we love your Word in scripture. It is a guide and comfort and inspiration. Blow your Spirit on the pages we read, and enliven them with your goodness, your love, your humour, that in understanding, we might know your intentions for our world. Amen.

TO THINK ABOUT: What do you love most about the Bible? How would you complete the sentence "The Bible is..."?

TRISHA ELLIOTT

SINGING THE OLD, OLD STORY

Know that I am with you and will keep you wherever you go.
Genesis 28:10-17

Jacob is for me not a wrestling patriarch, but a four-year-old with whom I spend some time every week. They call it grandparenting. When the situation calls for superior grandparenting skills—at bedtime or in the middle of the night—I make up new verses for "We Are Climbing Jacob's Ladder." My hope is that somewhere down the road he'll hear it and say, "Hey, that's my song." I want my song to become his song.

"Scripture is our song for the journey," the song that comforts and encourages, soothes and shocks. A song that tells us who we are: children of a loving Presence, never forgotten, always drawn in by big-armed welcome. We sing it to ourselves in order to bring us back to ourselves, especially when night seems too close, even for big people. Sometimes it's as simple as recalling the verses someone else has written. Other times we have to write our own new verses to the old tune.

Scripture is our song, written by others for us, by which we sing ourselves to knowingness and wisdom. Here we get to know a pilgrim God who walks with us, draws close to us, and will never abandon us. It takes many ballads of many stanzas to tell such a long story of anger, hatred, and reconciliation, of loss and recovery, of life and death and life again. These songs are often so compelling that we can't stop ourselves from making them our own. If we haven't been there yet, we suspect we may be at some time in the future and we'll want to have something to sustain us in hard times.

How fortunate we are to have so many tales to tell, the songs so many women, men, and children have sung against threatening powers. And left space for us to add a few verses of our own.

HYMN: "I Was There to Hear Your Borning Cry" (*Voices United* 644)

PRAYER: God of song and story,
      We thank you for campfires and church pews
        and storytelling circles
      Where we hear the good news
        of your great love for us.
      Open our ears to your Word wherever we are,
      And give us the heart to understand
        What you are telling us. Amen.

TO THINK ABOUT: What part(s) of the Bible bring you life? comfort? challenge?

V. MARTYN SADLER

CHALLENGING CULTURAL EXPECTATIONS

Do not judge, and you will not be judged.
Luke 6:37, 38

Much of what we take from the Bible is based on the biases and cultural expectations of another time. For example, what many young people wear today would probably cause ridicule, horror, and even harassment in biblical times. I'm not saying that the current generation's pop culture models for the youth of today are wrong; the styles are reflections of our time that would be ridiculed in another era.

The same kind of cultural expectations are found in the church and are something of a pet peeve of mine. Once, after reading the evening's scripture at a nondenominational church, I was thanked by the minister for delivering the word of God. Okay, that's fine; I like a bit of encouragement as much as the next person. But then, as I was still moving toward my seat, the minister had the audacity to mention that even people with long hair and a shabby appearance can still help in ministering God's message. Whoa, back up. Shabby appearance?

Now, I'll admit that I'm not exactly the most fashion conscious person on the planet. I do not, generally speaking, care about what I wear as long as it prevents me from feeling cold or getting arrested. Sure, my clothes are not what one would want to be wearing to a formal or even a semi-formal event—or perhaps any gathering. But I digress. My point is that the minister expected a cookie-cutter, 1950s suit-and-tie appearance, with a "nice" haircut. Nothing wrong with that expectation, but expectations are just that—what you expect. Reality has a funny way of showing its love for us, does it not?

I guess what I'm trying to say is that people have to be careful about what they say about others, especially those in positions of authority. Churches (in general) need to be more accepting of those not fitting the norm, or they risk alienating them. *"God calls us to be doers of the word and not hearers only."*

To conclude my story, I left that church and, not long after, became an adherent of the United Church.

HYMN: "Just As I Am" (*Voices United* 508) or "Sisters, Let us Walk Together" (*More Voices*⁶)

PRAYER: O God, you made us all different and you called your creation good. Help us accept people as they are, even if they don't live up to our expectations. Help us to be patient and treat everyone with love and dignity. Amen.

TO THINK ABOUT: What are some assumptions about the church that we may have that are based in culture and tradition?

ROBERT PIKE

---

⁶ Hymn numbers for *More Voices* were not available at time of printing. *More Voices* will be available in Spring, 2007. Please refer to the first line index.

WHERE WE FIND HOPE

Rejoice in the Lord always.
Philippians 4:4-7

I will lift up my hands and call on your name.
Psalm 63:1-8

During the first two days of my ordained ministry, I was called to minister at a funeral for a 16-month-old toddler who had been tragically killed in an automobile accident. Through the days leading up to the funeral, my eyes welled with tears a lot, my heart hung on prayers uttered in sighs too deep for words, and my arms reached out for extra hugs from and for my own kids.

Not only was I filled with deep sorrow for the family of that small child, I was overwhelmed with a deep anxiety about having to be the one who would attempt to speak a word of hope in the face of that community-wide tragedy. I remember going to the 1969 United Church *Service Book* for some guidance. It seemed strikingly odd to me that it would instruct me to include, near the start of the funeral service, the singing of a hymn "setting forth the greatness and goodness of God." I wondered how we could possibly draw forth strength to praise God when our hearts were so heavy with grief. I worried, too, that instead of praise, many in the congregation would want to extend blame.

But as we began to sing "Praise to the Lord, the Almighty" on that day of remembrance, our weak and quiet voices began to fill with strength and hope. Even through our tears, people who were bent down from the steely weight of sorrow were able to stand straight.

I learned some important lessons that day. We offer God our worship not only when we have hope, but when we need hope. I discovered that praising God isn't a solo activity; we do it with and for each other. And I experienced first-hand that when we rejoice in the Lord, it reminds us that even though our world may feel like it is spinning apart, God has not let go of us.

HYMN: "Praise, My Soul, the God of Heaven" (*Voices United* 240)

PRAYER: God, who rejoices in our joy and holds us in our sorrow, grant us strength to offer you our praise even in the hard times. May our grief be met with hope and our darkness with your light. Help us discover your peace which passes all understanding and guards our hearts and minds in Jesus Christ.

TO THINK ABOUT: When was the last time you were invited to offer praise to God even though you were not feeling up to the task? Were there others who lifted up praise on your behalf when you couldn't?

R. MARK GIULIANO

PREPARING TO WORSHIP

Remember the Sabbath day, and keep it holy.
Exodus 20:8-11

For those Sundays when I'm sitting in a pew preoccupied by when I should hold the next Wider Work meeting or what to have for supper, this is the kind of advice I would like to give myself...

For now, just worship. Worship with your whole heart. Sing loudly and joyfully. It doesn't matter if you sing off-key. As an old Scottish prayer says, give thanks to God that you have risen today to the rising of this life itself. And don't forget to include those smaller graces, like enough energy and good humour to get through your work, a child's sloppy kiss, a dog's friendly nuzzle, good talks, music, books, a lover's touch, the warmth of sun on your skin.

Carve out for yourself some small spaces of silence, and let the peace of God seep into your soul. Listen to the Eternal. Then really get your mind around the scriptures. Don't get bogged down in the violence and sexism of certain passages, but appreciate the Bible for what it is, an historical, indispensable, inspired witness to God's doings with the Hebrew people, to Jesus, and the early church. Let it speak to you.

Listen carefully to the words of the preacher. Those words are also used by and infused with the larger Word. Don't hesitate to pour out your heart to God, asking for forgiveness and guidance, and for those things you, those you love, and the world need most.

Enjoy the company of the saints in the next pew. Have some fun on this journey together. Finally, remember the Sabbath in the Jewish tradition, a time for rest and thanksgiving and to take delight in God, family (or those like family), good food, creation. It's a time to set aside the burdens of life and live as though the Kingdom has come, a foretaste of paradise. Savour the day, beginning with the joy of worship.

HYMN: "We Are One" (*Voices United* 402)

PRAYER: Praise to you God, Creator, Son, and Spirit, that you have given us the gift of this new day. Praise to you that you have blessed us with your presence and this company of your people, the church. Thanks to you that you sing with us in our joy, mourn with us in our loss, console us in our sorrow, steady us in our fear, and cheer us on to holier living.

TO THINK ABOUT: What do you find most meaningful and joyful about Sunday worship?

PATRICIA WELLS

WEEK FIVE *We Sing of Jesus*

*W*e find God made known in Jesus of Nazareth,
and so we sing of God the Christ, the Holy One embodied.

We sing of Jesus,
a Jew,
born to a woman in poverty
in a time of social upheaval
and political oppression.
He knew human joy and sorrow.
So filled with the Holy Spirit was he
that in him people experienced the presence of God among them.
We sing praise to God incarnate.

Jesus announced the coming of God's reign—
a commonwealth not of domination
but of peace, justice, and reconciliation.
He healed the sick and fed the hungry.
He forgave sins and freed those held captive
by all manner of demonic powers.
He crossed barriers of race, class, culture, and gender.
He preached and practised unconditional love—
love of God, love of neighbour,
love of friend, love of enemy—
and he commanded his followers to love one another
as he had loved them.

Because his witness to love was threatening,
those exercising power sought to silence Jesus.
He suffered abandonment and betrayal,
state-sanctioned torture and execution.
He was crucified.

But death was not the last word.
God raised Jesus from death,
turning sorrow into joy,
despair into hope.

We sing of Jesus raised from the dead.
We sing hallelujah.

By becoming flesh in Jesus,
    God makes all things new.
In Jesus' life, teaching, and self-offering,
    God empowers us to live in love.
In Jesus' crucifixion,
    God bears the sin, grief, and suffering of the world.
In Jesus' resurrection,
    God overcomes death.
Nothing separates us from the love of God.

The Risen Christ lives today,
    present to us and the source of our hope.
In response to who Jesus was
    and to all he did and taught,
    to his life, death, and resurrection,
    and his continuing presence with us through the Spirit,
we celebrate him as
    the Word made flesh,
    the one in whom God and humanity are perfectly joined,
    the transformation of our lives,
the Christ.

SUNDAY REFRAIN: CHOOSING TO BE WITH US

God is Holy Mystery,
beyond complete knowledge,
above perfect description...

We also speak of God as...
the One on whom our hearts rely,
the fully shared life at the heart of the universe.[7]

When I was young, I had a favourite aunt named Dotty. She would come to visit on birthdays and high holidays, swooping into our humdrum lives like a swirl of fireworks on the first of July. She always brought us presents and told us funny stories, and then, with a flourish, would get on the train, leaving us bereft...waiting for the next time.

But one summer, Auntie came for a whole month. And what a difference it made! She still brought us presents and told stories. But the difference was that we could tell her our stories. We could talk to her about what really mattered to us, what delighted us, what hurt us, and what hopes we had for the future. It was a magical summer: her spirit and the memories of those long walks and earnest conversations stayed with us for a long time.

Throughout the Bible, we read stories about God making the occasional visit to earth to see how things were going, whether walking in the garden at the dawn of creation (Genesis 3:8), appearing in a burning bush (Exodus 3:6), or speaking through an angel to a young girl in Nazareth. (Luke 1:20) What was new about the promise of the gospel was that God came to stay. And like the time my Aunt Dotty came to live with us for a whole month, it meant that God chose and God still chooses to listen to our stories and

---

[7] The full refrain from "A Song of Faith" appears on page 11.

to share our joys and sorrows. In *"the Word made flesh,"* we find someone who makes all the difference to our lives.

> And so we sing of Jesus, whose life, teaching, and self-offering
> empower us to live in love.
> Jesus, whose death and resurrection remind us again and again
> that God overcomes death
> and nothing will ever separate us from God's love.

HYMN: "O Love, How Deep" (*Voices United* 348)

PRAYER: Astounding God, we are amazed that you should choose
to be one of us.
We thank you for the gift of Jesus,
who walked among us, wept with the suffering,
and struck out with anger at injustice.
Help us walk in Jesus' way,
that we might share his joys and sorrows and grow in
our capacity to love.
We pray through the One who sings the Song and
shows the Way.
Amen.

TO THINK ABOUT: If Jesus were sitting beside you, what would you like to tell him?

NANCY E. HARDY

WHO IS JESUS?

For in him all the fullness of God was pleased to dwell.
Colossians 1:15-21

There is a lot of controversy about Jesus in our congregation these days. The debate is usually polite, impassioned, and, I think, constructive. The basic crunch is over whether Jesus was *"God incarnate"* or divine only to a greater degree than the rest of us. As one who sometimes finds herself in the lonely but traditional middle, let me weigh in with a few thoughts on this.

Whether Jesus regarded himself as uniquely one with God, we will never know, but certainly he saw himself as having the authority to command, to overrule the Law, and to forgive sins. He experienced himself as powerfully directed by the Spirit and had a very special personal relationship with his Abba, Father, or Daddy.

Within the church, his divinity was not an invention of the fourth-century councils that formulated the creeds. Very early Christians were already using extravagant titles for Jesus, such as Lord and Saviour (terms commonly applied to Caesar) because of their relationship to the One who had conquered death. The credal doctrines about Christ grew out of their ongoing experience of him in prayer, worship, and communal and everyday living. Those earliest believers asked, "If we praise and thank him, trust and hope in him, then who is he?"

If Jesus is just another highly spiritual man, then much of what we do as Christians today makes little sense. Only consider how we pray in Jesus' name, sometimes pray to him, and how we pray to "have the mind of Christ" so that we might be new creatures in him. We seek communion with him through the sacrament of bread and wine. Our most basic Christian belief has been that "God was in Christ reconciling the world to [God]." Through Jesus' death and resurrection, God transformed decisively and for all time the relationship between God and humanity, between God and the whole of creation. The cross stands at the centre of our faith. It is only if Jesus was indeed "the fullness of God" that all we do as Christians holds together.

HYMN: "The Love That Clothes Itself in Light" (*Voices United* 137) (alternate tune: O WALY WALY at VU 372)

PRAYER: Suffering God: As we stand again at the foot of the cross, we are appalled at the misery we see there. We know how completely you were one with this man and so this is not simply another victim of a cruel regime. This is you, Creator God, who are experiencing and absorbing into yourself the pain and suffering of the world. In an act as mysterious as creation, you are reconciling us and all that is to yourself. And we are in awe that you love us this much. Amen.

TO THINK ABOUT: How would you explain to someone who is asking about your faith that, in the crucifixion of Jesus, *"God bears the sin, grief, and suffering of the world"*?

PATRICIA WELLS

KNOWING JESUS

This is my commandment, that you love one another as
I have loved you.
John 15:12

I have a more distant relationship with Jesus than some. The avalanche of words written about him gets in the way, I think, as do television evangelists. You stumble over someone saying "Jesus saves," and you know they mean only "their Jesus"—for everyone.

God is not so difficult. There's something about immanence. Jesus may get captured by television or someone's too-familiar conversation, but God is in and through and transcending all things. God can be addressed in any place, like under my maple tree. I lie there and whisper to the tree and to God that I love this shade, this music of leaves, this coolness in the hot summer, thank you.

So the take on Jesus in "A Song of Faith" is important to me. Yes, it involves more words; but they are simple and clean and not insistent that I, a) stop thinking, and b) try to convert my Jewish friends. In fact, these words about Jesus are, above all, sensible: he is a Jew who—like other great sages before him, Jeremiah and Ezekiel, the Buddha, Euripides, Confucius—taught us *"peace and justice."* He commands us to love one another, which threatens the principalities and powers, and so he is killed. But *"nothing separates us from the love of God,"* and therefore he is risen. Hallelujah!

This Jesus loves my maple tree, the vine and fig tree of Canadians. This Jesus wants everyone to live in peace and enjoy the summer shade. This Jesus knows that the way to that peaceable kingdom is still blocked by *"those exercising power,"* still threatened by *"his witness to love."* Wars are fought for the sake of the oil on which wars run, the polar ice caps melt, and the poor whom Jesus loves suffer.

But—says "A Song of Faith"—that is not the end of the story. The Risen Christ is alive today, *"present to us and the source of our hope."*

This Jesus is my brother and my friend.

Hymn: "There in God's Garden" (*Voices United* 346)

Prayer of Intercession:
> God of Nazareth and Bethlehem
> God of impoverished people and of glaciers and trees
> Grant us peace.
> Water the fields of the poor with your good rain
> Water the hearts of the rich with your compassion
> In the name of Jesus who loves us all anyway. Amen.

To Think About: What does knowing Jesus mean to you?

Donna Sinclair

WHAT WOULD JESUS DO?

Blessed are you who are poor, for yours is the kingdom of God.
Luke 6:20-26

"Hi, how are you doing?" I asked. "I'm all right," said the old
man looking up warily from the filthy clothes he was spreading
out on the picnic table. He had also laid out a few coins, a loaf of soggy
bread, a watch, and several grocery bags. "It really stormed last night,"
I commented. "All my stuff's wet," he answered haltingly as though
unaccustomed to conversation, "Lightning hit this tree right here around
two o'clock." "You were out here all night? It was the biggest storm of the
year! Where did you sleep?" I asked, remembering how a particularly close
flash of lightning sent my son and me scurrying to the basement. "Under
the pavilion here until it really rained hard. 'Bout one o'clock I went to
the toilets." "The outhouse? You slept in the outhouse?" "Least it was dry."
"Weren't you scared out here all alone?" He laughed. "No. I was scared
when a guy held a knife to my throat once. No, storms don't scare me."

"He crossed barriers of race, class, culture, and gender."

"Where are you headed?" I asked. "Morrisburg," he answered. "I grew up
in Morrisburg," I said. "It could take you a couple hours to bike there and
it's supposed to be 90 degrees today. I could give my husband a call on my
cell if you'd like a lift. We can put your bike in the back of the van." "No
thanks," he said.

"He healed the sick and fed the hungry."

"Well, at least let me give you 20 bucks to buy yourself a good lunch. You'll
need the energy," I offered. "No thanks. I've got bread here and I've got
money," he declined. "Are you sure?" "Yup."

"He preached and practised unconditional love—"

"Well, is there anything I can do?" I asked. "No. I'm fine. Just glad to meet you," he said.

"We celebrate him as the Word made flesh, the one in whom God and humanity are perfectly joined."

"My name's Trish." "Mine's John." (And two hands, one raw and dirty, the other soft and manicured got a grip on each other.)

HYMN: "Lord Jesus, You Shall Be My Song" (*Voices United* 641)

PRAYER: Jesus, light of the world; Jesus, sword of truth, you convict us with your presence and convince us to work in your way. Guide us, encourage us, and push us for your sake and the sake of the world. Amen.

TO THINK ABOUT: How does this story reflect the kind of encounters Jesus had with people? Are there times when you've offered help to people and found it was not the kind of help they needed?

TRISHA ELLIOTT

FOLLOWING JESUS

Everyone will know that you are my disciples, if you have love for one another.
John 13:33-35

"Juh-ee-sus!" That's how the name "Jesus" sounded when I heard it spoken in Nashville, Tennessee, almost 15 years ago. I thought that the three-syllable Jesus was just a Southern thing until I moved to London, Ontario, and heard a minister pronounce his name with the same drawl. I wondered whether the preacher had picked it up at a conference or from television. It seemed like another example of an American version of Christianity imposing itself beyond the borders, or at the very least, the Canadian church adopting an American (read: free market, growth) model.

But it wouldn't be the first time Jesus was co-opted for ecclesial, political, or even personal gain. (Does Jesus really want us to be rich?) And lately, we stamp the "Jesus seal of approval" on everything from our dirty little wars, to political candidates (Who Would Jesus Vote For?), and even to the kind of car we drive. (Walk with Jesus, Drive a Prius!)

In the church, our sweet Jesus sometimes conveniently blesses our latest faith statement, hymn book, or theology. Although our spiritual world might be opened up a bit by being an eco-feminist, Gaia worshipping, Buddhist-Wiccan-Christian, I am not sure I am comfortable arguing that Jesus was one. I am not sure I am even comfortable with the term "Christian" anymore. I opt for the less offensive, and yet more descriptive, "disciple of Jesus." It's less about our Jesus religion and more about our relationship with Jesus. The religion embroidered on our golf shirt matters a whole lot less than the name Jesus Christ inscribed on our hearts.

What is important is that we pick up the cross every day and follow where Jesus has gone, namely, to that selfless, die-on-a-cross love for God and world. Jesus invited us to live the abundant life, not the fearful life. He didn't call us to make mega churches or even institutional religion. Thank Constantine for that. No, Jesus told us to wash each other's feet.

HYMN: "They'll Know We Are Christians"
or "Jesu, Jesu" (*Voices United* 593)

PRAYER: God of grace and mystery, you have come to us in the most human of ways. You walked among us; you healed the sick and fed the hungry; you called us to reach beyond the boundaries and love God and neighbour with our whole being. As a servant, you spoke truth to power and changed the course of history. In this world of anxious and self-centred preoccupations with fulfillment and greed, teach us how to be servants like Jesus, that we might truly live in the abundance of your love. Amen.

TO THINK ABOUT: Whose feet have you washed this week?

R. MARK GIULIANO

CHALLENGING THE EMPIRES

He has brought down the powerful from their thrones, and lifted up the lowly.
Luke 1:46-55

Visitors are led through the narrow alleys between the wooden shacks of Navotas, a shanty-town in the port of Manila. Children come running, laughing, shouting to greet them. Seeing the African among them, they run to find a missing playmate: "Come and see your uncle!" She is the child of a Filipino mother and a Ghanaian father. She is thrilled to be photographed with the Black man. In the photo he stands proudly beside her, holding her hand. She is no longer alone. There is another like her. The smile will last all day.

When Jesus comes to slip his hand into ours, we feel God's presence beside us. So this is the way the Creator made us! Isn't that something! The child is delighted to see the original. The Creator recognizes in us the goodness originally intended and is not ashamed to be known by us. We know we have a place. God smiles on us.

God sends the man Jesus to speak and be a piece of God's government in exile. In him God challenges the empires of this world, in which the strong succeed and the rich prosper. In the alternative empire, the ruler lifts up the humble, feeds the poor, and ensures that peasants have land to own and farm, and schools for their children. Not so much a challenge as a contradiction.

The slighted child is raised up and honoured. In this moment she is a new person, seen by others in a new light. Jesus has that effect on people: on those in the picture and out of it, looking on. This is the way the world is meant to be, we say to ourselves, when we hear the story and see the picture. God's empire is breaking through to surprise us in the strangest places.

HYMN: "like a child" (*Voices United* 366)

PRAYER: O God, we thank you for Jesus,
    voice for the poor
    and hope for the voiceless.
  We thank you that in him
  Our world is turned upside down and
    becomes the way you intended.
  Help us listen; help us follow; help us believe. Amen.

TO THINK ABOUT: How does Jesus turn the world upside down? How does he affect your life?

V. MARTYN SADLER

Seeing the Whole Picture

No one has ever seen God. It is God the only Son, who is close to the Father's heart, who has made him known.
John 1:18

By becoming flesh in Jesus,
God makes all things new…

Nothing separates us from the love of God.
"A Song of Faith"

As directed by the Bible, Christians believe in an omnipotent God. God is loving, kind, and compassionate. We know God traditionally as the Father, but there are many names which God also bears, all of which are applicable.

There is also the Son, Jesus Christ, God's Holy Spirit made known to us in human form. He came to us and gave his own life for the redemption of our sins.

Finally, the scripture tells of the Holy Spirit itself. Acting through us whenever three or more are gathered in prayer, we find the Spirit to be continuing truth even in our time.

The power of these three, the Triune God, empowers us to be faithful servants and adherents to Christianity. While we may fail in our duties from time to time, we are nonetheless welcomed back, so long as our regret for our deviations are genuine. From this simple principle, one can draw much strength in times of trial.

HYMN: "Jesus, Come to Our Hearts" (*Voices United* 324)

PRAYER: God of many names,
> you come to us as Creator, Christ, and Spirit.
> Give us ears to hear your will for us;
> give us eyes to see what the world needs from us.
> Help us to grow in trust
> and know you are always with us,
> so we can better reach out to others in your name. Amen.

TO THINK ABOUT: How often do we remember, in times of difficulty, that God is always with us and on our side? How can we strengthen this trust?

ROBERT PIKE

WEEK SIX *We Sing of a Church*

We sing of a church
    seeking to continue the story of Jesus
    by embodying Christ's presence in the world.
We are called together by Christ
    as a community of broken but hopeful believers,
    loving what he loved,
    living what he taught,
    striving to be faithful servants of God
    in our time and place.
Our ancestors in faith
    bequeath to us experiences of their faithful living;
    upon their lives our lives are built.
Our living of the gospel makes us a part of this communion of saints,
    experiencing the fulfillment of God's reign
    even as we actively anticipate a new heaven and a new earth.

The church has not always lived up to its vision.
It requires the Spirit to reorient it,
    helping it to live an emerging faith while honouring tradition,
    challenging it to live by grace rather than entitlement,
for we are called to be a blessing to the earth.

We sing of God's good news lived out,
a church with purpose:
    faith nurtured and hearts comforted,
    gifts shared for the good of all,
    resistance to the forces that exploit and marginalize,
    fierce love in the face of violence,
    human dignity defended,
    members of a community held and inspired by God,
        corrected and comforted,
    instrument of the loving Spirit of Christ,
    creation's mending.
We sing of God's mission.

We are each given particular gifts of the Spirit.
For the sake of the world,
   God calls all followers of Jesus to Christian ministry.
In the church,
   some are called to specific ministries of leadership,
   both lay and ordered;
   some witness to the good news;
   some uphold the art of worship;
   some comfort the grieving and guide the wandering;
   some build up the community of wisdom;
   some stand with the oppressed and work for justice.
To embody God's love in the world,
   the work of the church requires the ministry and discipleship
   of all believers.

In grateful response to God's abundant love,
   we bear in mind our integral connection
   to the earth and one another;
we participate in God's work of healing and mending creation.
To point to the presence of the holy in the world,
   the church receives, consecrates, and shares
   visible signs of the grace of God.
In company with the churches
   of the Reformed and Methodist traditions,
we celebrate two sacraments as gifts of Christ:
baptism and holy communion.
In these sacraments the ordinary things of life
—water, bread, wine—
point beyond themselves to God and God's love,
   teaching us to be alert
   to the sacred in the midst of life.

Before conscious thought or action on our part,
   we are born into the brokenness of this world.
Before conscious thought or action on our part,
   we are surrounded by God's redeeming love.
Baptism by water in the name of the Holy Trinity
   is the means by which we are received, at any age,
   into the covenanted community of the church.

It is the ritual that signifies our rebirth in faith
and cleansing by the power of God.
Baptism signifies the nurturing, sustaining,
and transforming power of God's love
and our grateful response to that grace.

Carrying a vision of creation healed and restored,
we welcome all in the name of Christ.
Invited to the table where none shall go hungry,
we gather as Christ's guests and friends.
In holy communion
we are commissioned to feed as we have been fed,
forgive as we have been forgiven,
love as we have been loved.
The open table speaks of the shining promise
of barriers broken and creation healed.
In the communion meal, wine poured out and bread broken,
we remember Jesus,
we remember not only the promise but also the price that he paid
for who he was,
for what he did and said,
and for the world's brokenness.
We taste the mystery of God's great love for us,
and are renewed in faith and hope.

SUNDAY REFRAIN:
SEARCHING FOR COMMUNITY

God is Holy Mystery,
beyond complete knowledge,
above perfect description.

Yet,
in love,
the one eternal God seeks relationship.[8]

L ast year, I moved to the city where I now live. With a move, there are always too many tasks to count: locate the nearest grocery store, find a new doctor, a new dentist, a new optometrist, a new…. Oh yes, and find a new church: for me, the most difficult task.

So I began the search. The churches were impressive: magnificent buildings with beautiful stained glass; well trained, dedicated choirs; brave and imaginative outreach programs; thoughtful preaching.

"What are you looking for?" asked a friend. After considerable reflection, I realized that my search wasn't necessarily about great preaching or highly professional music. I was looking for relationships. I was looking for a place I could call home: a place where people knew my name and cared about me; where I was welcomed at Christ's table and felt part of a congregation that welcomed and included everyone, regardless of colour, race, sexual orientation, or age; where worship was a mix of the traditional and contemporary, with drama and dance alongside preaching and prayer.

I also knew instinctively that it wasn't enough to attend a church just for worship and a chat at the coffee hour. The church, which is the body

---

[8] The full refrain from "A Song of Faith" appears on page 11.

of Christ, is called to care for the hurt and the hungry and confront the powers that keep the hurt and the hungry in their place. The church is called to witness to the good news of Jesus Christ in word and action.

The good news for me is that I found a church I could call home. And to my wonder and delight, it was filled with people I recognized. Because they were like you and me: sinful, forgetful, forgiven. Together, we're involved in caring for one another and the world. Together, we sing of meaning and mission. We sing thanksgiving for God's gift of church.

HYMN: "God Is Here" (*Voices United* 389) or Psalm 78 (VU page 792)

PRAYER: We thank you for your church,
    Christ's body of celebration, compassion, and cooperation.
  We thank you for the variety of people and gifts that come
    together in your name.
  Forgive us when we become self-righteous and impatient
    with one another;
  Help us work for the common good.
  We pray through Christ, our foundation. Amen.

TO THINK ABOUT: What is your experience of church? What would you wish for if you were looking for a new church community?

NANCY E. HARDY

A WORD FITLY SPOKEN

Clothe yourselves with compassion.
Colossians 3:12-17

One Sunday following worship, our small community of faith in west Nashville had gathered around tables laden with an abundance of fine Southern cooking: fried chicken, sweet potato pie with loads of brown sugar and whipped cream, baked beans, butter beans, and pecan pie. Our cups were overflowing with sweet tea as I've tasted only in the South. At the table where I was sitting though, there was a friend, Mike*, who could hardly eat a scrap. He was lamenting how much his life sounded like the country and western songs he sometimes wrote for a living. He said, "I lost my job, my wife, and my kids. And to be honest, right now, I feel like I've lost my faith."

A little part of my clergy heart jumped as I rifled through files of pastoral theology in my brain, desperately searching for the right words to offer him. But one of our Elders, a young woman named Ann*, beat me to it offering the perfect response with wise words that have stayed with me ever since. Ann said, "Mike, that's okay. Until you get through this, we'll believe for you." Mike choked back some tears. With a hug, he thanked her. And then he picked up his fork and started eating. No wonder Proverbs 25:11 reads, "A word fitly spoken is like apples of gold in a setting of silver."

At its best, the church is the community that believes for one another, hopes for the world, and regularly gathers around a Word and a Table to be nourished for the rocky road of faith and the servant ministry of all. The image of God within us is never clearer, and we are never more Christ-like than during those times when we bear the cross for one another.

*The names have been changed.

HYMN: "We Are Pilgrims" (*Voices United* 595)

PRAYER: God of healing and renewal, who pieces us together with a word fitly spoken, who knits us together around a table of mercy and binds our hearts as one in the fellowship of grace, we offer you thanks and praise for the blessings of our faith community. Help us to strengthen and support one another along the journey. As we seek to be imitators of Jesus, reveal your image within us with glowing clarity.

TO THINK ABOUT: Who needs your prayers today? What will you do to support them?

R. MARK GIULIANO

LIVING OUT THE GOOD NEWS

Like living stones, let yourselves be built into a spiritual house.
1 Peter 2:5

I have lived in this United Church all my life and I am fiercely proud of it. In the struggle through the gay ordination debates, I watched people lining up at the microphones at General Council, weeping their way to a just conclusion. Years later, when a further debate incurred similar emotions, this time over gay marriage, I saw hundreds fall silent while a young woman, trembling, described her two mothers and how much she loved them. And then they voted to support equal marriage.

I have seen this church wrestle with its fear over apologizing for the residential schools (would this bankrupt the church?) and finally—none too soon—follow the path of repentance to its end and say "We're sorry."

This church has such a history: Victoria Cheung, getting a medical degree, going to South China in 1923, surviving wars and rebellion, and healing, healing, in our name; Lucy Affleck—six years after Cheung had sailed to Kong Moon—losing her job for raising the alarm about Native residential schools; Ernie Best, conscientious objector, sailing against the temper of the times during World War Two to teach interned Canadian citizens of Japanese origin; Norman Bethune; Bob McClure; Jim Endicott; John Webster Grant; Willie Blackwater; and Jessie Oliver, calling us to repentance, making us whole.

Our list of heroes goes on and on, and each of them comes out of a congregation where Sunday after Sunday they read the gospel and sing hymns and pray. Week after week, in small towns and large ones, the people gather and remember their ancestors and look to the future, trying to be "*a blessing to the earth.*" Trying their very best to be, as "A Song of Faith" promises, "*God's good news lived out.*"

I know there are many paths to God, and Christians know but one of them. But this is my path, my church, my home, my heart.

HYMN: "As a Fire Is Meant for Burning" (*Voices United* 578)

PRAYER OF BLESSING:
>Blessings for the ancestors behind us
>Blessings from the angels above us
>Blessings on the work that's before us
>Blessings to the earth that's beneath us
>Blessed by the love that's among us.
>Blessed by our church. Amen.

TO THINK ABOUT: Can you call your church your home, your heart? How is it (or how can it be) like that?

DONNA SINCLAIR

A Place of Faith

Now you are the body of Christ and individually members of it.
1 Corinthians 12:27-31

More and more I am finding that the United Church is an important part of who I am. I have no doubt that this journey of mine, seeking deeper connection with the church, will not stop anytime soon. The church is a valuable resource for me: it is a place of both relaxation and study; it is a place where any questions I have will more than likely get addressed—I am free to ask any question of faith without reprimand.

As a place of faith, the church is where I may learn from the amassed teachings that can be found in the Bible and from theologians of this time. More than that, it is a place that actively seeks to make its material presentable and applicable to many different people, who may be at different points in their lives so that certain messages will ring true for them more so than others.

"A Song of Faith" also speaks of the church as a community where everyone is connected. In my experience, I have seen that the United Church is welcoming of new members, seeking not only to "bring them into the fold," but also recognizing the gifts that each new person brings to the church and showing a willingness to incorporate these gifts into worship and study.

The United Church respects other forms of Christianity, recognizing that it is neither "the right way" nor "the only way." The church also does much in the way of interfaith work: the lines of communication are open so that all parties may know more about the varying belief systems of our world. In my limited experience with the three biggest churches in Canada, only the United Church has embraced openness to diversity to such a degree.

This church offers praise and worship, fellowship, education, community, and willingness to embrace diversity, as well as a genuine commitment to working towards a better, more sustainable world. If this church does not embody some of the qualities that I assume God would want, then I would be hard pressed to find one that does!

Hymn: "The Church Is Wherever God's People Are Praising" (*Voices United* 579)

Prayer: O God, we thank you for your church where we can be ourselves and connect with others in our search for you. We thank you for its respect for others and for the way it reaches out to the world. Help us work together, that we can grow together and serve the world. Amen.

To Think About: In what ways can we work to better the church within our own communities?

Robert Pike

MARINATING OUR SOULS

O come, let us sing to the Lord;
let us make a joyful noise to
the rock of our salvation!
Psalm 95

Sooner or later, the confirmation class will get to worship, and I'll trot out the word "marinate." It may not increase understanding at first, but they sit up and pay attention.

Worship, the marinade for the perfecting of Christians, has several ingredients in it—water, wine, salt, spices, and herbs. It tenderizes hardened hearts. It adds flavour and appeal to jaded lives. It takes time; it can't be hurried. Once a week, Christians feel the need to come and soak up something of God's goodness. Standing in the presence of God, telling God our stories, and listening to the stories of others and their encounters with God, eating together as guests of Jesus, we absorb into our beings the attributes of God. We start to take into our lives forgiveness, generosity, courage, and passion for life.

I cling to this image because it helps me through the dry times, the spiritless prayers, the aimless sermon—especially when I'm the one leading worship. This is an activity we shouldn't have to justify as we go out the door, ticking off hymns sung, scriptures heard, bread eaten, wine drunk. It's not that functional. Who can tell how that experience has reshaped me and my fellows for the week ahead?

It's the reshaping I keep going back for. I go to open my senses to God in hopes that God can get right into the fibre of my being and put me back on the street a changed person. I'm not asking that hamburger become top grade beef, but I'm trusting God's marinade will improve the quality. Nothing can withstand a good marinade—not cucumber, carrot, steak, or human being.

What would become of me if I stopped dropping in and giving God another chance to change me? God, the marinater of my being. Those kids may laugh, but they remember.

HYMN: "As a Chalice Cast of Gold" (*Voices United* 505) "Spirit, Open My Heart" (*More Voices*[9])

PRAYER: Savoury God,
> You flavour our lives and permeate our hearts,
>> and we are changed for the good.
> Thank you for worship
>> where we can be steeped in your enlivening Word
>> and empowered by your Spirit.
> Help us always to be open to your grace. Amen.

TO THINK ABOUT: What are you hoping for when you go to worship? What will you offer?

V. MARTYN SADLER

---

[9] Hymn numbers for *More Voices* were not available at time of printing. *More Voices* will be available in Spring, 2007. Please refer to the first line index.

MEETING CHRIST IN THE ORDINARY

For all of you are one in Christ Jesus.
Galatians 3:23-28

It was a typical day at the beach. My four-year-old son and I were building sandcastles, skipping rocks, holding hands as we walked down the dock, skin wrinkling in the cold river water. Out of nowhere there were songs: French and African. One of them I recognized: "Kum Ba Yah." The water froze and then parted as swimmers instinctively stopped and then separated and scurried to shore. My son and I stood in a huddle with others on the beach; we looked on curiously. We were about to witness a baptism.

A young girl, maybe 10, wearing white robes, followed the pastor into the water. The singing grew louder: "Hallelujahs!" were accompanied by clapping and swaying. It was joyously rhythmic. I couldn't help clapping along. A statuesque elderly woman in a black and gold patterned gown with matching hat turned to those of us standing on the sidelines. "Join us," she waved, never breaking tune. We stood among them, dripping from our gaudy beach towels, humming a foreign tune, clapping an unknown rhythm. Our music became a shield for the private words spoken between pastor and parishioner before they went under.

The sacrament of baptism I experienced that day was a powerful witness, not only of faith, but of inclusiveness. There was no Black or White, no English or French, no us or them. We stood together. One church. One faith. One God. We gathered *as Christ's guests and friends. In holy communion...* Those of us who had gone to the beach just to swim that beautiful summer morning were welcomed to meet Christ there. There were no questions asked, no stipulations made, nothing about age or belief, just invitation upon invitation. "Come and stand with us." "Come and sing." "Come and celebrate." And, "Come by here, my Lord! Come by here!"

That, to me, is what sacraments are all about—gracious offerings that rise alongside other believers and greet Christ in ordinary things made extraordinary.

HYMN: "All Who Hunger" (*Voices United* 460)

PRAYER: God of Font and flowing water, God of Cup and Open Table, we come to you, knowing that we belong, that we are welcome to meet the Christ who stands, arms open to all of us. Amazing love! Touch us with your blessing and grant us peace and courage. Amen.

TO THINK ABOUT: When do you feel most included in the life of the church? How can the sacraments of baptism and communion be made even more welcoming and inclusive?

TRISHA ELLIOTT

THE CHURCH UNIVERSAL

Go therefore and make disciples of all nations.
Matthew 28:16-20

One of the most remarkable things I've discovered about the church over the years is its universality. Whether worshipping in Korean, or Norwegian, or Basotho congregations, I have felt thoroughly at home among people who share my beliefs. With some justification, overseas mission and missionaries are generally held in disrepute these days. But the fact is that without the enormous sacrifice, dedication, and courage of those same missionaries, the church would be a much smaller and declining Western institution, instead of the vibrant, global movement it is.

Let me tell you an abbreviated story about one distant church I knew and loved well, the Church of Lesotho...

Eugene Casalis was a 19-year-old French missionary with the Paris Evangelical Missionary Society. In 1833, he and two young friends set out for Cape Town with no clear idea of where they were going. God was calling them and God would show them the way. From the Cape they travelled northward, looking for a tribe to evangelize. Meanwhile, Moshoeshoe, the Paramount Chief of the Basotho, found his people threatened by encroaching Dutch and British settlers. He had heard that missionaries could be politically useful and he badly needed advice on how to keep his territory intact. He sent a scout to the south, looking for a missionary; the scout duly returned with the young French men.

Casalis later wrote that he found the small, rounded, mud huts claustrophobic and the diet of cornmeal and greens monotonous and barely nourishing. The ways of the Basotho were often baffling and disturbing, and he laboured to learn the language. But Casalis knew what he was doing. His mission was to evangelize, educate, and help keep the country (which later became Lesotho) free of White settlers—all of which Casalis was able to accomplish.

Saturday 🍂 *Day 34*

Although today Lesotho is very poor and seriously weakened by AIDS, it has the decided advantage of possessing a highly literate and independent population, with government leaders of integrity who are the direct spiritual descendants of Casalis. The Church of Lesotho itself is thriving and an integral part of the worldwide ecumenical church body.

HYMN: "In Christ There Is No East or West" (*Voices United* 606)

PRAYER: Lord, when we as a church start hunkering down into a clubhouse mentality, bring us up short. Remind us that you have a mission for us and so call us to be the church to get the job done. We need direction, Lord, and the wisdom to know how best to serve a world hungry for peace, bread, and meaning. Help us to support one another and find strength in you, as together we work to make a difference in your world.

TO THINK ABOUT: How do you see yourself and your congregation participating in God's ongoing mission to bless creation?

PATRICIA WELLS

DAILY REFLECTIONS FOR LENT   107

HOLY WEEK *We Sing of God Our Hope*

We place our hope in God.
We sing of a life beyond life
   and a future good beyond imagining:
   a new heaven and a new earth,
   the end of sorrow, pain, and tears,
   Christ's return and life with God,
   the making new of all things.
We yearn for the coming of that future,
even while participating in eternal life now.

Divine creation does not cease
   until all things have found wholeness, union, and integration
   with the common ground of all being.
As children of the Timeless One,
   our time-bound lives will find completion
   in the all-embracing Creator.
In the meantime, we embrace the present,
   embodying hope, loving our enemies,
   caring for the earth,
choosing life.

Grateful for God's loving action,
   we cannot keep from singing.
Creating and seeking relationship,
   in awe and trust,
we witness to Holy Mystery who is Wholly Love.
Amen.

SUNDAY REFRAIN: THE CRUCIFIED WOMAN

God is Holy Mystery,
beyond complete knowledge,
above perfect description...

We witness to Holy Mystery that is Wholly Love.[10]

I always look for her when I go to Emmanuel College in Toronto. She hangs alone, outside the back doors, as students and staff pass by.

"The Crucified Woman," a sculpture of a naked, suffering woman, was created by Almuth Lutkenhaus-Lackey and presented to Emmanuel in 1986. Prior to finding its way to the college, the sculpture hung in the chancel of Bloor St. United Church. At the church, as well as the college, the Woman evoked passion, pity, and joy. Some wept and found liberation from their suffering and a new understanding of Christ's crucifixion. Some were troubled; some were offended by her nakedness.

There's no doubt about it. For many, the sculpture was shocking, even scandalous. A crucified woman? A naked body in the courtyard of a theological college? One night, partying students dressed her in coloured crepe paper (security came regularly on party nights). But still she hung there, her body rebuking us, reminding us of Jesus, who also hung naked on a cross, a scandal to all who passed, some to jeer, and some to weep.

God's love, the light of the world, slowly being extinguished.

Last fall, as I hurried to a meeting, I looked for her again and discovered that the garden that had been created for her had grown around her, dressing her in birch green leaves and softening the lines of her suffering body. A garden, enclosing her with hope of new life.

---

[10] The full refrain from "A Song of Faith" appears on page 11.

At the beginning of Holy Week, our thoughts turn to the passion of Jesus, the suffering One whose cross was chosen out of love. Life and love poured out for all of us, even those of us who hurry by. Crucifixion, yes, but also Resurrection. Because Holy Week leads us to a garden where Jesus' suffering and shame is transformed, and rising, he beckons us to "*a future good beyond imagining.*" At the end of this week, we know we will find that garden, an emptied tomb, and life beyond life.

Hymn: "When I Survey the Wondrous Cross" (*Voices United* 149)

Prayer: Suffering God,
    As we begin this Holy Week,
    Help us be aware of the loneliness of abandonment
      and the despair of those around us who suffer from
      violence, hunger, and homelessness,
      even as we meditate on the passion of Jesus.
    Surround us with your Spirit,
      and shine your hope on our path
      as we begin our way to Calvary.
    We pray in the name of Jesus Christ, crucified and risen.
    Amen.

To Think About: What are the crosses being raised today, in our own lives, in the world?

Nancy E. Hardy

AFFIRMING LIFE

For I am about to create new heavens and a new earth.
Isaiah 65:17-19

I second guessed myself as I stepped up to the door. Should I have brought him? Would the wiggling and squawking be a bother? Would my baby be too much for a dying man?

But I knew that Jack had a soft spot for children so I went ahead and made an impromptu pastoral visit with my infant son, Aidan. When Jack broke into a smile and took hold of Aidan's hand, I knew it was a good thing.

It was one of those death-defying, flowers-at-the-funeral, and emptiness-filling, casserole-after-the-reception moments. A real life-in-life, life-after-life affirmation. A sacred stitch in time where the "here and now" collides with the "yet to come." And I was privileged to see God's activity first-hand. In the space between Aidan and Jack's skin, there was God. God was in the gap, rubbing a little heaven on earth and a little earth on heaven until the line between where's where, what's what, and who's who grew hazy.

And something became clear: God is not so much heaven's keeper as heaven's planter, and so I should not be so concerned with whether I'll be in or out at some future gated moment, as with whether I'm growing more holy in the open here and now.

Early the next morning, Jack died. I got the call. "I'll be right there," I said. And no sooner had I arrived and sat down than the family shared: "Aidan was his last visitor."

They could have said that I was his last visitor. They could have said that Aidan and I were his last visitors. They didn't. Although I had visited with the authority of my office, with holy intention, and with prayer upon my heart, it was clear to everyone that during that visit I was close to but not the closest thing to God. God was there, in bed. In the exchange of a baby and man. Somewhere between the drawing and unveiling covers.

HYMN: "In the Bulb There Is a Flower" (*Voices United* 703)

PRAYER: God of mystery and eternity, you slip between the lines of life and remind us that you are with us in life and in death, and in life beyond death. Thank you for your constant presence and your love. Thank you for surrounding us with your hope and grounding us in your Spirit. We trust in you. Amen.

TO THINK ABOUT: How might the death of a loved one help us to see God in that moment? How might Holy Week direct your thoughts to matters of life and death and life beyond life?

TRISHA ELLIOTT

MAKING OUR WORLD
A BETTER PLACE

*"Truly I tell you, just as you did it to one of the least
of these who are members of my family, you did it to me."*
Matthew 25:31-40

*In the meantime, we embrace the present,
  embodying hope, loving our enemies,
  caring for the earth
choosing life.*
"A Song of Faith"

This passage serves as a reminder that we should not be so focused on "earning our spot" in heaven that we neglect our responsibilities in our own realm.

We have been promised a place of paradise, our reward for good deeds done while on earth. Yet sometimes, with the busyness of everyday life, it gets difficult to remember that those good deeds need to be done through the generosity of our heart, not carried out seeking and expecting a reward. In particular, it is hard to remain generous in our dealings with other people since, as a species, we tend to be self-centred. Making sacrifices can be challenging at times, but by no stretch of the imagination is it impossible.

Sometimes, I am reminded that a small effort on our part can help make someone's day. This is enough to motivate me. Consider a time when a friend did something for you that made your day feel much better— perhaps a simple gesture or action. Now consider how little the effort that simple gesture required compared with the boost it gave you.

I am again reminded of Charles Mackay and his water analogy about human effort. (See Wednesday of Week Two, page 32.) Even the smallest action can help someone, somewhere. I find that few things in life are futile as long as genuine effort is involved. In working to make our friendships and commitments stronger, we are, in turn, making our communities stronger, rooted in the virtues the Creator wishes us to follow.

HYMN: "Make Me a Channel of Your Peace" (*Voices United* 684)

PRAYER: God of this time and the next, we thank you for the
hope you give us of a better world. We thank you that we
can make a difference and pray that we will sense your
presence in what we do. Help us walk in your way. Amen.

TO THINK ABOUT: In what ways can you work to better this world before moving into the next?

ROBERT PIKE

ENCOUNTERING THE TIMELESS ONE

God said to Moses, "I AM WHO I AM."
Exodus 3:13-15

There is a word that I trip over in my speech and public speaking classes. It's easy enough to pronounce; it's a simple, one syllable word, only three letters long. If you spell it backwards, it can be as playful as a puppy. Yet the word itself is laden with the weight of thousands of years of distortion, manipulation, and corruption. No wonder when some hear it spoken, it can whip up a storm of anger or hostility. And yet, for others, the word can signify ultimate truth, abiding peace, or never-ending love. The word is God.

At times, the word is an insufficient term that attempts to designate a huge, benevolent, and eternal presence. I remember the first time I had an encounter with the Timeless One, though at the time I had no words to name it.

I was seven years of age. It was night. I was lying in a snowdrift outside of my childhood home in exurban Toronto. Our road hockey game had come to a grinding halt when every kid in the neighbourhood had been called in to do homework or finish chores.

I don't know why I didn't go in. I just remember falling backwards, gently, into that snowdrift. Maybe to make an angel. Maybe to have a rest. Maybe to avoid chores. I do remember that I wasn't cold. I wasn't afraid. And I wasn't alone. I was, however, overwhelmed with a mysterious sense of peace and a connectedness with the universe as I stared up into the night sky. It felt, to me, for the very first time, as if all of us, my family, friends, neighbours, the entire world itself, were enveloped in a wonderful, glowing dome of love.

I didn't have a word for what I experienced that evening, but I do today. It is God. But for me, God is not only a being, but also a place, a home, a stillness in our hearts that binds together in this giant snow shaker in which we live.

HYMN: "Immortal, Invisible, God Only Wise" (*Voices United* 264)

PRAYER: O wise and beautiful Timeless One, you are as distant as the farthest star and as close as our own breathing. You fail to fit our moulds, our boxes, our narrowly defined parameters. Thank you. In vulnerability and mystery, you allow the infinite to enter the world of the finite. You have torn the curtain that separates you from us. Enable us to stand before you not in fear, but in awe.

To Think About: What do you hear when you hear the word God?

R. Mark Giuliano

In the Meantime...

We do not live to ourselves, and we do not die to ourselves.
Romans 14:7-9

It hit me several months ago. I am going to die. Not soon, I hope. But some day.

There is no reason I can think of for this revelation. I just got up one morning and looked out the window and ached with the loveliness of the day. And then I thought, I don't know how many are left, these gentle spring days with the new green rising everywhere, the rock phlox bursting into bloom. It wasn't even sunny. It was a gardener's day, windless with a misty rain. You can plant anything in this weather, and it'll be fine.

But I know now that every day is shining. I may be allowed another 30 years of days, please God, with family all about, "the founding children," as one grown-up son calls them, and my grandchild too.

Or none. No more days at all.

"A Song of Faith" speaks of *"life beyond life."* It tells me not to fear, and I don't. It promises *"a future good beyond imagining: a new heaven and a new earth…completion in the all-embracing Creator."*

(But what, I wonder, could be better than this present moment?)

The Song anticipates that thought. *"In the meantime,"* it says, *"we embrace the present…caring for the earth, choosing life."*

Fine, then. For the days that remain to me, I will choose life. I will care for this planet earth—the part that is my garden and the part where I canoe, and the parts that are damaged and ugly and sore. I will fling compost about the perennials and visit my grandson. I will write to newspapers and carry placards. I may even wear a funny hat and—with my sisters—sing wicked songs in public to politicians who disappoint us. I will work in elections and plant many, many trees.

And on Sundays I will walk down the hill to church. We will pray and read the gospel and visit one another. So I will witness to *"Holy Mystery who is Wholly Love."* I cannot keep from singing.

HYMN: "Give Thanks for Life" (*Voices United* 706)

PRAYER OF CELEBRATION:
> Hallelujah, Timeless God,
> I sing to the day you have created
>   and the night.
> The music of your wind hums through the noisy trees, the poplars.
> And everything grows—moose and deer, wolves and bear,
>   water lilies, bulrushes, wheat, spruce, potatoes, tomatoes, roses.
> I sing to it all, Timeless One,
> and to the stardust I will one day be.
> Hallelujah, Timeless God. Amen.

TO THINK ABOUT: What is there about life that gives you hope and keeps you singing?

DONNA SINCLAIR

BLESSED ASSURANCE

But if we have died with Christ, we believe that we will also live with him.
Romans 6:1-11

As I hear again the narrative of Jesus' last days, I wonder how Jesus saw it all. When he set out for Jerusalem, did he expect to end up on a cross? Was his commitment to die on a cross or was it to keep faith with God's project, God's reign in our world? He must have known that death was a possible outcome. What did he think lay beyond the sorrow, pain, and tears?

God, I suppose. I mean, he expected God lay on the other side of death. Could he have hoped for anything less than that? For anything more? Like most Christians I know, I allow for a lot of latitude in the furnishings of heaven. I don't want to interfere in other people's flights of fancy, but my hope is pinned on God and nothing more.

I imagine that for most of us the more important question is life *before* death, life here and now in the shadow of so many little deaths. We've lived through the loss of loved ones, friendships, marriages, careers, congregations, dreams. That's when we turn to God and ask to see new life for ourselves and the others who walk with us. Show us life, God, right here, right now! That's what we want, isn't it?

Still, even as God tugs us towards wholeness, we know we'll never see it fully exposed in our lives. We take to heart the assurance that the One who stands outside history will accomplish, has already accomplished, the *shalom* we long for. Yes, even in the midst of great suffering and sorrow, we cling to this, that the victory is won, and we're already celebrating the fullness of God's justice. Yes, even as a just and gentle man is led out to be crucified.

HYMN: "He Came Singing Love" (*Voices United* 359)

PRAYER: O God, on this Good Friday
>   we think of Jesus suffering on a cross
>   for our sake,
>   and the sake of the world.
>   And yet we also know of his victory
>   and his triumph of good over evil.
>   We praise you for his life, death, and resurrection.
>   We praise you for hope and the assurance
>   that your reign of *shalom* shall come to pass. Amen.

TO THINK ABOUT: How did God bring life from the crucifixion? How does God bring us new life?

V. MARTYN SADLER

LOOKING TO THE LIGHT

*"Death will be no more; mourning and crying and pain
will be no more, for the first things have passed away."*
Revelation 21:1-6

In the dim beginning
of human time
a woman leans over a grave,
carefully placing a spear
and bowl of wild grain
by her husband's side,
knowing the bones, bowl, spear
will remain in the dirt
but signalling a hope
that his spirit will rise
into an embodied paradise.

In a clear blue dawn
the women are dancing
down the road,
laughing, arms raised,
fingers snapping,
feet light in the
cool morning dust,
gleeful that their rabbi
and friend
has escaped the cruelty of Romans,
Sadducees, and Death,
by a shimmering miracle,
a divine sleight of hand,
freed into a future
of God's choosing,
hopeful that where
he has gone
they one day may follow.

HYMN: "Love Divine, All Loves Excelling" (*Voices United* 333)

PRAYER: God of New Beginnings: we wonder again at your ability to bring life out of nothing, your capacity to set nature and nations on edge and open all the world's windows to spring. We give thanks for the resurrection promise that, at death, we will not fall into a void of nothingness, but will be embraced by you, who in this life has loved us so well. We thank you for this assurance that the future of our world is, finally, in your loving hands.

TO THINK ABOUT: How would you explain your own belief in "*life beyond life*"?

PATRICIA WELLS

SUNDAY REFRAIN: WE CANNOT KEEP FROM SINGING

God is Holy Mystery,
beyond complete knowledge,
above perfect description...

Nothing exists that does not find its source in God.[11]

Preparing a sermon the Easter following my husband's death was one of the most difficult things I did in my pastoral ministry. How could I sing a happy hallelujah in my grief? How could I sing at all?

Maybe I couldn't sing, but I could preach, and I was determined to let my people know what the resurrection was all about. There were to be no cute stories, no flights of fancy: I would make it all clear. I began my preparation by diligently reading the Easter scripture passages and commentaries and scanning my favourite authors. That didn't help. It didn't explain the mystery.

But one morning, as I pondered the death and rising of Jesus Christ, I recalled John Shelby Spong's take on the story of the Upper Room that first Easter evening (see John Shelby Spong's *The Easter Moment* HarperCollins, 1987). Like me, the disciples were grieving, and there would have been no hallelujahs in their lexicon. But they broke bread together, and then, to their amazement and wonderment, Christ was there! Christ was there, and they knew he was still part of their lives. They knew that his Love would never die.

Life beyond life! Could it happen to me as it happened with the disciples? Of course it could. I had been privileged to have a profound relationship

---

[11] The full refrain from "A Song of Faith" appears on page 11.

with an interesting, intelligent man, and that relationship did not die when he did. In the Upper Room, Christ showed the disciples that there was indeed life beyond life. By doing so, Christ gave all of us hope: hope of new life beyond death; hope of loneliness transformed by memories; awareness of a Spirit who gives us faith and strength to carry on.

And so, on Easter morning, I told the story of the Upper Room. I shared my own experience of the mystery of the resurrection—the darkness and pain of death, the first timid steps into the light of the garden, the certainty of enduring love. And I proclaimed the hope and the joy of knowing that I was not alone—the risen Christ was with me in my tears and in my new beginnings. Hallelujah!

Grateful for God's loving action,
 we cannot keep from singing.

Creating and seeking relationship
 in awe and trust,
we witness to Holy Mystery who is Wholly Love.
Amen.

HYMN: "Joy Comes with the Dawn" (*Voices United* 166)

PRAYER: Great and glorious God,
   You turn our mourning into gladness,
   And call us from night into a shining dawn.
   We praise you for your great Love
     and for the risen Christ
     who brings us new life.
   We ask for an awareness of your Spirit
     this day and every day. Amen.

TO THINK ABOUT: What are some resurrection moments in your life?

NANCY E. HARDY

GUIDE FOR STUDY GROUP LEADERS

Singing a Song of Faith can be the basis for some lively discussion and faith sharing. The following are outlines of group meetings that can take place in a hall, a Sunday school room, or someone's home. If you're forming a new group, or if there are newcomers in a continuing group, provide name tags for everyone for the first few meetings, so all will feel an equal part of the group.

Set out some norms for your life together. They can be prepared ahead of time with the participants invited to comment and suggest additions. Some possibilities are:

1. **Be honest:** say what you're thinking and feeling and not what you think the group wants to hear.
2. **Listen to one another:** sometimes this may mean that someone holds back from "having all the ideas" (even if it means holding back some really good ideas).
3. **Never laugh or ridicule another's opinions:** the group needs to be a safe space for everyone.
4. **No one should dominate the conversation (especially the leader):** conversation should be shared fairly around the group. If the group is large, break up into two's and three's from time to time so everyone gets a chance to speak.
5. **Agree to disagree sometimes:** be aware that we are talking about matters of faith and there is not always one "right" answer to the questions under discussion. Unanimity within the group may not be possible.

ONE WAY IN

THE BASIC GROUP MEETING (about 60 minutes)

1. Sing

Each reflection in *Singing a Song of Faith* ends with a hymn suggestion (or more than one suggestion). Your group might begin by singing these hymns and also singing their own favourites.

You might also adopt a "theme hymn" that expresses the many facets of our Christian faith and that can be sung at the beginning of each meeting, e.g.: "God of the Sparrow" (*Voices United* 229), "The Singer and the Song" (VU 248), or "When in Our Music, God Is Glorified." (VU 533)

2. Check-in

Give each person a minute or two to share about their personal life, or a question related to the theme for the week. (See the suggested questions in the "Week by Week" section that begins on page 129.)

3. Think about the Text

Together read the refrain (page 11) from "A Song of Faith," and then invite someone (or two or three people) to read the section from "A Song of Faith" that forms the basis for the week's reflection (pages 13, 23, 41, 57, 73, 91, and 109). Think about it in silence for a minute or two, and then talk about it. What did you like about it? What was difficult to understand? Which reflection did you find most helpful? What would you like to say to the writers? (See other questions in the "Week by Week" section.)

4. Close with Prayer

Ask the participants to name people or events to pray for, then pray in silence. Close with a prayer that the leader has written or collected, or use the prayer in "Week by Week."

In each section of "Week by Week," you will also find "Another Way In," which suggests some creative activities your group might also like to do.

WEEK BY WEEK

Week One: We Sing of God the Creator

Additional Hymns:
"I Sing the Mighty Power" (*Voices United* 231), "All Creatures of Our God and King" (VU 217), "All Praise to You" (VU 297), "Called by Earth and Sky" (*More Voices*[12]), "Deep in Our Hearts" (MV)

Check-in Questions: (use one)
• Why have you decided to become part of this group?
• What part of God's creation do you find most appealing? Most troubling?

Questions for Reflection:
1. What does it mean to say that we "*live and move and have our being in God*"?
2. Trisha Elliott talks about the importance of affirming our bodies because we are created in the image of God. What effect does popular culture have on the way we see ourselves and others?
3. How are all parts of creation, "*animate and inanimate*," related?
4. How can we find right relationships with each other and with God?

Closing Prayer:
Creating God, we give you thanks that you have made us out of love
  and set us on this earth to live in harmony and peace.
We thank you for signs of spring—
  for golden daffodils and purple crocuses, melting snow and flowing water,
  for all of your good and beautiful creation, and for our part in it.
We pray that
  we might grow in love for one another
  both at home and throughout the world,
  cherishing and nurturing all you have given us.
Help us to sing your song in gratitude,
  even as we are surrounded by signs of your creative goodness.
We pray through Jesus Christ, the Singer and the Song. Amen.

---

[12] Hymn numbers for *More Voices* were not available at time of printing. *More Voices* will be available in Spring, 2007. Please refer to the first line index.

ANOTHER WAY IN

1. Begin a series of banners that illustrate "A Song of Faith." Each week, assemble materials for people to create a banner that combines the "song" for the week with a symbol or picture. For example, this week's banner would be titled "We Sing of God the Creator." It might incorporate a symbol of creation, such as a tree, an animal, a gardener.
or
Create a very large piece of art with the heading "Singing a Song of Faith." Each week, add a "song" and a symbol.

2. Give each person a journal (a blank notebook) in which they can record their thoughts and reflections at the end of each meeting. Give them a couple of questions each week to start them off. Your questions for Week One might be: What does it mean for me "*to live and move and have [my] being in God*"? What was the best (or most challenging) part of being in this group today?

Week Two: We Sing of Grace

Additional Hymns:
"Great Is Thy Faithfulness" (*Voices United* 288), "Lord, Listen to Your Children" (VU 400), " Come, Let us Sing of a Wonderful Love" (VU 574), "When Quiet Peace Is Shattered" (VU 615), "Psalm 89: My Song Forever Shall Record" (VU page 804), "Don't Be Afraid" (*More Voices*); "Kyrie Eleison (Oré poriajú)" (MV)

Check-in Questions: (use one)
• What is your favourite kind of music?
• If you were in charge of the world, what would you fix first?

Questions for Reflection:
1. What does it mean to say that we yearn for life in God, but choose to surrender ourselves to sin?
2. Find examples from our world and from your own personal life to illustrate each of the sins listed in this week's section. Now identify some experiences of God's grace that have affected you in some way.

3. How does personal sin become part of the way we live as individuals or as a culture?
4. Donna Sinclair finds God's grace in communion (see page 38). Where do you find God's grace in worship?

Closing Prayer:

Gracious and Merciful God,
We thank you for your grace and for your patience
    with our brokenness;
We thank you for your persistent love in the face of all we do
    to hurt one another and your world.
Help us be reconcilers
    as you have reconciled us in Jesus.
Help us work with you
in the healing of the world.
We pray through Christ, who comes reconciling and making new. Amen.

ANOTHER WAY IN

1. Work on the banner project. Symbols for this week might include a flower, candle, a broken chain.
2. Questions for the journal: How am I part of the world's brokenness? What was the best (or most challenging) part of this meeting?
3. Write a group prayer of confession that might be used in your church's worship service. A suggested outline:
    Merciful God, (Patient Mother-Father God, Tender Spirit, Healing Creator), we confess our brokenness: we are sorry for (*name situations in personal lives, in neighbourhood, in the world*).
    We thank you for...
    We pray in the name of.... Amen.

Week Three: We Sing of God the Spirit

Additional Hymns:
"Like the Murmur of a Dove's Song" (*Voices United* 205), "Holy Spirit, Hear Us" (VU 377), "The Lone, Wild Bird" (VU 384), "Dance with the Spirit" (*More Voices*)

Check-in Questions: (use one)
- Tell us something about your name.
- Tell us about a time when you felt God's presence in your life.

Questions for Reflection:
1. What are some different ways we name and think about God's Spirit?
2. What has been your experience of God's Spirit—something that "knocks you off your feet" (Elliott, see page 48), or "a moment of pure sensation" (Pike, see page 53), or something different?
3. In what ways is the Spirit challenging for us?
4. How does the Spirit transform us and our world?

Closing Prayer:
Spirit of truth, come as the wind to refresh us
   and renew our strength to do your will;
Spirit of power, come as fire to kindle our hearts
   and encourage us;
Spirit of gentleness, come as a still, small voice
   and open us to the cries of the world.
Come, Holy Spirit.
Surround us and hold us,
Push and enliven us,
Help us to be aware of your presence
In all we say and do
That we may live for the love of God and neighbour. Amen.

ANOTHER WAY IN
1. Work on the banner project. A symbol for this week might be: a heart, a spiral (symbolizing wind), a circle of friends.

2. Questions for the journal: How is God's Spirit working in my life? What was the best (or most challenging) part of this meeting?

3. Make a group collage about the work of the Spirit in the world. Have on hand a sheet of newsprint, magazines, newspapers, scissors, glue, glitter glue, etc. Ask group members to find stories and pictures that illustrate communities working for justice, striving for change, living in harmony.

Week Four: We Sing of Scripture and Worship

Additional Hymns:

"Oh Sing a New Song" (*Voices United* 241), "Asithi, Amen" (VU 431), "Great God, We Sing That Mighty Hand" (VU 529), "Spirit, Open My Heart" (*More Voices*)

Check-in Questions: (use one)

- What does the word trust mean to you?
- What is your favourite book or passage from the Bible?
- What is your favourite part of worship?

Questions for Reflection:

1. *"Scripture is our song for the journey."* In what way has scripture been both a help and a stumbling block for people of faith throughout the years?
2. How does the Bible have power to affect the way you live?
3. How do you prepare yourself for weekly worship? What do you offer?

Closing Prayer:

Loving God,
You come to us in the living Word we call scripture.
Thank you for your wisdom, distilled over the years
    and brought to us by teachers and leaders
    and our own understanding.
Thank you for coming to us in worship,
    where we can praise you in song and dance
    and listen for your Spirit in prayer.

We pray that our speaking and living
   will reach out to the world
   and bring your Word honour and gratitude. Amen.

ANOTHER WAY IN

1. Work on the banner project. A symbol for this week might be: a Bible, a scroll, a lamp.
2. Questions for the journal: What Bible passages or stories are important in my life?
   What was the best (or most challenging) part of this meeting for me?
3. Spend some time talking about the way we read and understand the Bible. Then role play this situation: you have just been to a wedding, and the groom fainted. Have people act out what happened from the point of view of the mother of the bride, a close friend of the groom, the minister, and one of the attendants. Then, read together the story of Jesus being called the Messiah, found in each gospel (Matthew 16:12-20; Mark 8:27-30; Luke 9:18-21). What are some major differences in the way this incident is recorded? Why might this be so? What does it mean to say that we take the Bible seriously, but not literally?

Week Five: We Sing of Jesus

Additional Hymns:

"Lord Jesus, You Shall Be My Song" (*Voices United* 641), "Blessed Assurance" (VU 337), "Jesus Christ Is Waiting" (VU 117), "Three Things I Promise" (*More Voices*)

Check-in Questions: (use one)

• What qualities do you look for or hope for in a friend?
• What is your favourite story of Jesus?

Questions for Reflection:

1. *"We sing of God the Christ, the Holy One embodied."* What does it mean when we say that Jesus is the Word made flesh?

2. Patricia Wells (Monday; see page 78) and Donna Sinclair (Tuesday; see page 80) have quite different concerns when it comes to Jesus. How would you define those concerns? Which reflection most nearly expresses your faith?

3. Trisha Elliott tried to act as Jesus would when she met an old man spreading his worldly goods on a picnic table (see page 82). How do you respond to her actions? What would you have done?

4. "It wouldn't be the first time Jesus was co-opted for ecclesial, political, or even personal gain" (Mark Giuliano; see page 84) What does that mean? How do you react to Mark's statement?

Closing Prayer:

Gentle Jesus,
We come to you with thanks for your companionship and comfort
   and for your stories of healing and compassion;
Faithful Jesus,
We remember with gratitude your courage and suffering
   for the sake of the world;
Strong and wise Jesus,
We are mindful and grateful for your anger in the face of oppression
   and encouragement for all to act justly.
Risen Christ,
We praise you for your continuing presence
   and for the hope you bring us.
Teach us to walk in your way of both suffering and joy. Amen.

ANOTHER WAY IN

1. Work on the banner project: a symbol for this week might be a pair of sandals, a cross, a pair of hands.

2. Questions for the journal: What does knowing Jesus mean to me? What was the best (or most challenging) part of this meeting?

3. Look through *Voices United* and find hymns that describe Jesus in different ways, e.g. : "Fairest Lord Jesus" (VU 341), "Christ Is Made the Sure Foundation." (VU 325) Which hymn describes Jesus best?

Week Six: We Sing of a Church...God's Good News Lived Out

Additional Hymns:
"Come, Let Us Sing" (*Voices United* 222), "Worship the Lord" (VU 401), "Let Us Talents and Tongues Employ" (VU 468), "Bread of Life" (*More Voices*), "Go Make a Diff'rence" (MV)

Check-in Questions: (use one)
- Tell us about an outstanding event (happy or sad) from your past week.
- What do you think the church does best?
- Where do you feel you are most at home in the church?

Questions for Reflection:
1. What does being part of The United Church of Canada mean for you?
2. What part of church life do you find most life-giving?
3. How do you react to Martyn Sadler's description of worship as the perfect "marinade for the perfecting of Christians?" (see page 102)
4. What is most important about the two sacraments of baptism and communion?

Closing Prayer:
God of community,
We thank you for your church.
We thank you, that in spite of our failings,
we can still come together in prayer and praise.
We are grateful for the place we call home,
   where we belong, washed in the waters of baptism
   and welcomed at Christ's table.
We pray that we might be your courageous, strong people
   working for unity and peace,
   caring for those who are hungry and homeless,
   bringing your love to those who long for new life.
We pray through Christ, who is our sure foundation. Amen.

ANOTHER WAY IN

1. Work on the banner project. A symbol might be: a chalice, a teapot (or coffee mug), a globe of the world.
2. Questions for the journal: What does being part of the church mean to me?
   What was the best (or most challenging) part of this meeting?
3. Draw a picture of a perfect church, one that illustrates meaning and mission. Share your vision with the group.

Holy Week: We Sing of God Our Hope

Additional Hymns:
"What Wondrous Love Is This" (*Voices United* 147), "I See a New Heaven" (VU 713), "We Know That Christ Is Raised" (VU 448), "My Life Flows On" (VU 716), "Draw the Circle Wide" (*More Voices*), "There's a River of Life" (MV)

Check-in Questions: (use one)
• What have you learned (or gained) from being part of this group?
• How does having faith make a difference to your life?

Questions for Reflection:
1. In what way does Holy Week make us think more about life and death?
2. What are some ways in which we place our hope in God?
3. What does the phrase *"life beyond life"* mean for you?
4. How can we *"embrace the present"* even while having hope of a new heaven and a new earth?

Closing Prayer:
Holy God,
In this holiest of all weeks,
We come together with awe and sadness
    for the suffering and love that will be poured out
    for our sakes and the sake of the world.

But our sadness is softened by our knowing
   that you will bring hope out of mourning
As you raise Jesus Christ from the dead.

As you are with us in our sorrowing,
Be with us in our gladness and our knowing
   that there is life beyond life.
Thanks be to you, our Creator, our saviour, the ground of our being,
   our loving God.
Amen.

ANOTHER WAY IN

1. Work on the banner project. A symbol might be: a crown of thorns, a sunrise, a heart surrounded by a circle.
2. Questions for the journal: Who is Jesus Christ for me? Where is God in my life? What has been most helpful (or challenging) about being part of this group?
3. Share stories of what "A Song of Faith" has meant for the group. Prepare a closing prayer of thanks: have each person contribute a sentence that begins "For...," and follow each sentence with a group response: "we give you thanks," or "we praise your name," or "*we cannot keep from singing.*"

A SONG OF FAITH

A Statement of Faith of
The United Church of Canada/L'Église Unie du Canada

God is Holy Mystery,
  beyond complete knowledge,
  above perfect description.

Yet,
in love,
the one eternal God seeks relationship.

So God creates the universe
  and with it the possibility of being and relating.
God tends the universe,
  mending the broken and reconciling the estranged.
God enlivens the universe,
  guiding all things toward harmony with their Source.

Grateful for God's loving action,
we cannot keep from singing.

With the church through the ages,
we speak of God as one and triune:
Father, Son, and Holy Spirit.
We also speak of God as
  Creator, Redeemer, and Sustainer
  God, Christ, and Spirit
  Mother, Friend, and Comforter
  Source of Life, Living Word, and Bond of Love,
  and in other ways that speak faithfully of
the One on whom our hearts rely,
the fully shared life at the heart of the universe.

We witness to Holy Mystery that is Wholly Love.

God is creative and self-giving,
   generously moving
   in all the near and distant corners of the universe.
Nothing exists that does not find its source in God.
Our first response to God's providence is gratitude.
We sing thanksgiving.

Finding ourselves in a world of beauty and mystery,
   of living things, diverse and interdependent,
   of complex patterns of growth and evolution,
   of subatomic particles and cosmic swirls,
we sing of God the Creator,
the Maker and Source of all that is.

Each part of creation reveals unique aspects of God the Creator,
   who is both in creation and beyond it.
All parts of creation, animate and inanimate, are related.
All creation is good.
We sing of the Creator,
   who made humans to live and move
   and have their being in God.
In and with God,
   we can direct our lives toward right relationship
   with each other and with God.
We can discover our place as one strand in the web of life.
We can grow in wisdom and compassion.
We can recognize all people as kin.
We can accept our mortality and finitude, not as a curse,
   but as a challenge to make our lives and choices matter.

Made in the image of God,
we yearn for the fulfillment that is life in God.
Yet we choose to turn away from God.
We surrender ourselves to sin,
   a disposition revealed in selfishness, cowardice, or apathy.
Becoming bound and complacent
   in a web of false desires and wrong choices,
   we bring harm to ourselves and others.
This brokenness in human life and community
   is an outcome of sin.

Sin is not only personal
 but accumulates
 to become habitual and systemic forms
 of injustice, violence, and hatred.

We are all touched by this brokenness:
 the rise of selfish individualism
  that erodes human solidarity;
 the concentration of wealth and power
  without regard for the needs of all;
 the toxins of religious and ethnic bigotry;
 the degradation of the blessedness of human bodies
  and human passions through sexual exploitation;
 the delusion of unchecked progress and limitless growth
 that threatens our home, the earth;
 the covert despair that lulls many into numb complicity
 with empires and systems of domination.
We sing lament and repentance.

Yet evil does not—cannot—
 undermine or overcome the love of God.
God forgives,
 and calls all of us to confess our fears and failings
 with honesty and humility.
God reconciles,
 and calls us to repent the part we have played
 in damaging our world, ourselves, and each other.
God transforms,
 and calls us to protect the vulnerable,
 to pray for deliverance from evil,
 to work with God for the healing of the world,
 that all might have abundant life.
We sing of grace.

The fullness of life includes
 moments of unexpected inspiration and courage lived out,
 experiences of beauty, truth, and goodness,
 blessings of seeds and harvest,
  friendship and family, intellect and sexuality,
 the reconciliation of persons through justice

and communities living in righteousness,
and the articulation of meaning.
And so we sing of God the Spirit,
who from the beginning has swept over the face of creation,
animating all energy and matter
and moving in the human heart.

We sing of God the Spirit,
faithful and untameable,
who is creatively and redemptively active in the world.

The Spirit challenges us to celebrate the holy
not only in what is familiar,
but also in that which seems foreign.

We sing of the Spirit,
who speaks our prayers of deepest longing
and enfolds our concerns and confessions,
transforming us and the world.

We offer worship
as an outpouring of gratitude and awe
and a practice of opening ourselves
to God's still, small voice of comfort,
to God's rushing whirlwind of challenge.
Through word, music, art, and sacrament,
in community and in solitude,
God changes our lives, our relationships, and our world.
We sing with trust.

Scripture is our song for the journey, the living word
passed on from generation to generation
to guide and inspire,
that we might wrestle a holy revelation for our time and place
from the human experiences
and cultural assumptions of another era.
God calls us to be doers of the word and not hearers only.

The Spirit breathes revelatory power into scripture,
bestowing upon it a unique and normative place

in the life of the community.
The Spirit judges us critically when we abuse scripture
    by interpreting it narrow-mindedly,
    using it as a tool of oppression, exclusion, or hatred.

The wholeness of scripture testifies
    to the oneness and faithfulness of God.
The multiplicity of scripture testifies to its depth:
    two testaments, four gospels,
    contrasting points of view held in tension—
all a faithful witness to the One and Triune God,
the Holy Mystery that is Wholly Love.

We find God made known in Jesus of Nazareth,
and so we sing of God the Christ, the Holy One embodied.

We sing of Jesus,
    a Jew,
    born to a woman in poverty
    in a time of social upheaval
    and political oppression.
He knew human joy and sorrow.
So filled with the Holy Spirit was he
that in him people experienced the presence of God among them.
We sing praise to God incarnate.

Jesus announced the coming of God's reign—
  a commonwealth not of domination
  but of peace, justice, and reconciliation.
He healed the sick and fed the hungry.
He forgave sins and freed those held captive
    by all manner of demonic powers.
He crossed barriers of race, class, culture, and gender.
He preached and practised unconditional love—
    love of God, love of neighbour,
    love of friend, love of enemy—
and he commanded his followers to love one another
    as he had loved them.

Because his witness to love was threatening,

those exercising power sought to silence Jesus.
He suffered abandonment and betrayal,
    state-sanctioned torture and execution.
He was crucified.

But death was not the last word.
God raised Jesus from death,
    turning sorrow into joy,
    despair into hope.
We sing of Jesus raised from the dead.
We sing hallelujah.

By becoming flesh in Jesus,
    God makes all things new.
In Jesus' life, teaching, and self-offering,
    God empowers us to live in love.
In Jesus' crucifixion,
    God bears the sin, grief, and suffering of the world.
In Jesus' resurrection,
    God overcomes death.
Nothing separates us from the love of God.

The Risen Christ lives today,
    present to us and the source of our hope.
In response to who Jesus was
    and to all he did and taught,
    to his life, death, and resurrection,
    and his continuing presence with us through the Spirit,
we celebrate him as
    the Word made flesh,
    the one in whom God and humanity are perfectly joined,
    the transformation of our lives,
the Christ.

We sing of a church
    seeking to continue the story of Jesus
    by embodying Christ's presence in the world.
We are called together by Christ
    as a community of broken but hopeful believers,
    loving what he loved,

living what he taught,
striving to be faithful servants of God
in our time and place.
Our ancestors in faith
bequeath to us experiences of their faithful living;
upon their lives our lives are built.
Our living of the gospel makes us a part of this communion of saints,
experiencing the fulfillment of God's reign
even as we actively anticipate a new heaven and a new earth.

The church has not always lived up to its vision.
It requires the Spirit to reorient it,
helping it to live an emerging faith while honouring tradition,
challenging it to live by grace rather than entitlement,
for we are called to be a blessing to the earth.

We sing of God's good news lived out,
a church with purpose:
faith nurtured and hearts comforted,
gifts shared for the good of all,
resistance to the forces that exploit and marginalize,
fierce love in the face of violence,
human dignity defended,
members of a community held and inspired by God,
corrected and comforted,
instrument of the loving Spirit of Christ,
creation's mending.
We sing of God's mission.

We are each given particular gifts of the Spirit.
For the sake of the world,
God calls all followers of Jesus to Christian ministry.
In the church,
some are called to specific ministries of leadership,
both lay and ordered;
some witness to the good news;
some uphold the art of worship;
some comfort the grieving and guide the wandering;
some build up the community of wisdom;
some stand with the oppressed and work for justice.

To embody God's love in the world,
>   the work of the church requires the ministry and discipleship
>   of all believers.

In grateful response to God's abundant love,
>   we bear in mind our integral connection
>   to the earth and one another;
we participate in God's work of healing and mending creation.
To point to the presence of the holy in the world,
>   the church receives, consecrates, and shares
>   visible signs of the grace of God.
In company with the churches
>   of the Reformed and Methodist traditions,
we celebrate two sacraments as gifts of Christ:
baptism and holy communion.
In these sacraments the ordinary things of life
—water, bread, wine—
point beyond themselves to God and God's love,
>   teaching us to be alert
>   to the sacred in the midst of life.

Before conscious thought or action on our part,
>   we are born into the brokenness of this world.
Before conscious thought or action on our part,
>   we are surrounded by God's redeeming love.
Baptism by water in the name of the Holy Trinity
>   is the means by which we are received, at any age,
>   into the covenanted community of the church.
>   It is the ritual that signifies our rebirth in faith
>   and cleansing by the power of God.
Baptism signifies the nurturing, sustaining,
>   and transforming power of God's love
>   and our grateful response to that grace.

Carrying a vision of creation healed and restored,
>   we welcome all in the name of Christ.
Invited to the table where none shall go hungry,
>   we gather as Christ's guests and friends.
In holy communion
>   we are commissioned to feed as we have been fed,

forgive as we have been forgiven,
love as we have been loved.
The open table speaks of the shining promise
of barriers broken and creation healed.
In the communion meal, wine poured out and bread broken,
we remember Jesus,
we remember not only the promise but also the price that he paid
for who he was,
for what he did and said,
and for the world's brokenness.
We taste the mystery of God's great love for us,
and are renewed in faith and hope.

We place our hope in God.
We sing of a life beyond life
and a future good beyond imagining:
a new heaven and a new earth,
the end of sorrow, pain, and tears,
Christ's return and life with God,
the making new of all things.
We yearn for the coming of that future,
even while participating in eternal life now.

Divine creation does not cease
until all things have found wholeness, union, and integration
with the common ground of all being.
As children of the Timeless One,
our time-bound lives will find completion
in the all-embracing Creator.
In the meantime, we embrace the present,
embodying hope, loving our enemies,
caring for the earth,
choosing life.

Grateful for God's loving action,
we cannot keep from singing.
Creating and seeking relationship,
in awe and trust,
we witness to Holy Mystery who is Wholly Love.
Amen.

About the Writers

The Editor

The Rev. Nancy E. Hardy is a retired United Church minister who has served the church as a diaconal minister working in Christian education, mission study editor in the United Church's General Council Office, and ordained minister in several southern Ontario pastorates. She continues to combine editing and writing with her love of music and liturgy. Nancy edited the worship resource *Gathering* for three years and served as co-chair of the committee responsible for *Voices United*. She coordinates the Emmanuel College Newsletter and is a volunteer associate at Five Oaks Centre. Last spring, Nancy moved back to Toronto, a city she loves and calls home.

The Contributors

The Rev. Trisha Elliott is an artist and writer serving as the Christian Development Minister for Seaway Valley Presbytery, Montreal and Ottawa Conference. Prior to moving to Seaway Valley, she served the Glencoe-Appin Pastoral Charge in southwestern Ontario. She lives in Winchester, Ontario, with her partner, the Rev. Mike Perraul, and young children, Aidan and Isaac.

The Rev. R. Mark Giuliano teaches at the Savannah College of Art and Design, Savannah, Georgia, and is the author of numerous articles and publications including his most recent book *Speak Easy: The Survival Guide to Speech and Public Speaking*. A United Church of Canada minister, Mark is the pastor of Montgomery Presbyterian Church (USA) in Savannah. He is also a singer-songwriter of alternative and acoustic rock music. Check Mark's websites: www.rmarkgiuliano.com and www.marcusg.biz

Robert Pike is in his final year of secondary school. An Aboriginal person, he was reared in an environment where questions and answers were encouraged and sought. Robert is conscientious toward his family, his community, and his church. He loves the Creator and all that this entails— he knows his duties and responsibilities in living his life within Creation.

The Rev. V. Martyn Sadler is a retired United Church minister living in Sherbrooke (Lennoxville) in Quebec's Eastern Townships. He often shares in the leadership of worship at St. Mark's Chapel, Bishop's University.

Donna Sinclair's most recent book is *A Spirituality of Gardening*. With her husband, Jim, she lives in North Bay, Ontario, where she is working on *A Spirituality of Bread*, to be released this spring. Both books are published by Northstone.

Patricia Wells taught school in Lesotho where she served as overseas personnel for The United Church of Canada. Upon her return to Canada, she worked as a freelance writer and editor before becoming Staff Associate at East Plains United Church in Burlington, Ontario. Now retired, she is the doting grandmother of six grandchildren.